SpringerBriefs in Well-Being and Quality of Life Research

More information about this series at http://www.springer.com/series/10150

Youngwha Kee · Seung Jong Lee
Rhonda Phillips
Editors

Social Factors and Community Well-Being

 Springer

Editors
Youngwha Kee
Soongsil University
Seoul
Republic of Korea

Seung Jong Lee
Seoul National University
Seoul
Republic of Korea

Rhonda Phillips
Honors College
Purdue University
West Lafayette, IN
USA

ISSN 2211-7644   ISSN 2211-7652   (electronic)
SpringerBriefs in Well-Being and Quality of Life Research
ISBN 978-3-319-29940-2   ISBN 978-3-319-29942-6   (eBook)
DOI 10.1007/978-3-319-29942-6

Library of Congress Control Number: 2016934025

Printed on acid-free paper

This Springer imprint is published by Springer Nature
The registered company is Springer International Publishing AG Switzerland

Preface

Social factors traverse a large territory of impact and considerations. This volume seeks to explore several factors from the perspective of interaction, impacts, or outcomes on community well-being. It is at this intersection or nexus between social factors, policy, and impacts, and community well-being that insightful work is being done. The idea of influencing social factors and outcomes is of course not new; however, linking this to *community well-being* is a newer endeavor.

We begin this volume with Chap. 1, *Conceptualizing a Community Well-Being and Theory Construct* by HeeKyung Sung and Rhonda Phillips, presenting foundational concepts of well-being. The chapter looks at the relationship between community well-being and relevant theories, to present a construct for thinking about the dimensions inherent in well-being at this level of consideration. Building on theoretical approaches, a construct is offered that helps explain community well-being as a comprehensive concept covering other related life and community concepts. The term community well-being encompasses comprehensive and integrated concepts developed by synthesizing research constructs related to residents' perceptions of the community, residents' needs fulfillment, observable community conditions, and the social and cultural context of the community. Related terms such as well-being, happiness, and quality of life take on a crucial role in constructing community well-being. Community development in particular is explored by integrating related concepts, and major community components. The construct presented is inspired by well-established theoretical analysis such as systems theory, bottom-up spillover theory, social capital, and needs theory.

Next, Seung Jong Lee and Yunji Kim provide an overview of public services as a social factor and policy study in Chap. 2, *Structure of Well-Being: An Exploratory Study of the Distinction between Individual Well-Being and Community Well-Being and the Importance of Intersubjective Community Well-Being*. In this work, a comprehensive framework of well-being clarifies its meaning by distinguishing different types and aspects of well-being. Since public policy concerns public resources these aspects of community well-being are explored. Previous works only identified objective and subjective aspects of community well-being, leading to confusion in the measurement process regarding aggregation from individuals to the community. To address this issue, a third aspect called intersubjective community well-being measured by evaluative questions is identified. Using survey data from six districts in Seoul, South Korea, individual well-being and community well-being can be distinguished empirically and it is shown that the relationship between intersubjective and objective community well-being is stronger than the relationship between subjective and objective community well-being. This suggests that policymakers can gain better insight into policymaking by paying more attention to intersubjective community well-being, which effectively bridges relevant objective measures to collective evaluation of citizens.

Youngwha Kee and Chaebong Nam explore the aspects of community perceptions in Chap. 3, *Does Sense of Community Really Matter in Community Well-Being?* This chapter compares one vibrant grassroots community with its surrounding municipality in the context of subjective community well-being. Sungmisan is a small community formed from active community organizing and strong grassroots civic networks. It has similar objective conditions—in terms of local public services, or, objective community well-being—to those of its larger municipality host. Still, survey results show that Sungmisan residents were more satisfied with the local public services available in their community than were the municipal residents with theirs, suggesting that objective community well-being does not always determine subjective community well-being. Community-level characteristics, such as sense of community, appear to be the most likely differentiating influence. Sungmisan displayed high community-oriented characteristics, which was strikingly different from those of the larger municipality.

Geoffrey Woolcock's Chap. 4, *The Development and Production of Local, National, and International State of Children's Well-Being Report Cards*, presents the idea that local communities identifying and reporting on key indicators for children and young people is attracting significant attention as a model for many communities across the Asia-Pacific region. A number of these communities have leveraged their work through an association with the UNICEF Child-Friendly Cities model and/or government-funded place-based initiatives, all using various data and well-being reports as a foundational tool for their planning and monitoring. Other communities have looked to the enormous investment in standardized indices or national well-being scorecards to further the interest in how their own children and young people are faring. There is also a growing understanding internationally that 'place-based' and local responses are essential in responding to disadvantages and in promoting community well-being.

In Chap. 5, Sharan Merriam presents *Gender Equity and Community Well-Being*. It is argued here that attention to gender equity including the education and health of girls and women has a direct impact on numerous indicators of community well-being. Several international studies suggest that attention to gender equity creates human and social capital that enables community well-being. Human capital is the knowledge, skills, and health embodied in individuals and social capital refers to the patterns and qualities of relationships in a community characterized by norms of trust and reciprocity. Women's education has been linked to a reduction in infant and childhood mortality, socio-economic development, community development, physical and mental well-being, and so on. Attention to gender equity and in particular girls and women's education, leads to greater human and social capital which in turn leads to community well-being.

David Sloane and Hyunsun Choi explore the social factor of crime in Chap. 6, *Crime and Community Well-Being: The Role of Social Capital and Collective Efficacy in Increasing Safety*. Safety plays a central role in individual and community well-being. Scholars have long examined an individual's perception of their safety (subjective well-being) and the reality of crime (objective well-being) in their cities and towns. The role that safety has in affecting a community's sense of well-being at a neighborhood scale is explored. Positive community development requires that a neighborhood be safe. Improving safety is not just a role for the police and other governmental agencies. Instead, residents are important, even primary creators of safe neighborhoods in partnership with the criminal justice system. Critical to developing strong community actions to sustain safety are two relatively new concepts in sociology, criminology, and urban planning: social capital and collective efficacy. This chapter provides an exploration of the role these concepts play in increasing a community's sense of well-being through networking and connectivity, which leads to increased safety and happiness.

It is our intent that this volume will serve to spur interest in and more research on the subject of social factors and community well-being. The emergence of ideas and applications is happening rapidly and we sincerely hope this collection of research will be beneficial to supporting research at the beneficial intersection of social factors, policy, and well-being.

Youngwha Kee
Seung Jong Lee
Rhonda Phillips

Acknowledgments

This book was developed via research funded by the National Research Foundation of Korea, funded by the Korean Government (grant NRF-2013S1A3A2054622).

Contents

Editors and Contributors

About the Editors

Youngwha Kee is Professor in the Department of Lifelong Education at Soongsil University and president of the National Institute of Lifelong Education. She currently serves as the director of the Korea Institute of Local Development Education. Previously, Dr. Kee was president of the Association of Adult and Continuing Education of Korea and researcher of Korea Association for Community Education. She has served on several advisory committees in relation to educational policies and has been deeply involved with community education among multicultural families and education for the disadvantaged. She serves on the editorial board of the International Journal of Continuing Education and Lifelong Learning (Hong Kong)) and the Lifelong Education Magazine (Taiwan). Her research interests include older adult learning, community education, civic education, and community development.

Seung Jong Lee is a Professor at the Graduate School of Public Administration, Seoul National University and president of the Korea Research Institute for Local Administration. Previously, he served as the president of the Korean Association for Public Administration and as chief editor of several academic journals in related fields. He has frequently advised local and national governments through such positions as chairman of the Local Government Administration Joint Evaluation Committee, vice-chairman of the Presidential Committee on Local District Reorganization Plans, and member of the presidential transition committee. He has not only done extensive research on citizen participation and local autonomy, but has also been a strong advocate and educator in the field. He is the author of *Theories of Local Autonomy*, and *Democratic Politics and Citizen Participation.*

Rhonda Phillips is Professor in the Agricultural Economics Department and Dean of the Purdue University Honors College. Rhonda's honors include serving as a Fulbright UK Ulster Policy Fellow in Northern Ireland at the University of Ulster, and a Senior Specialist to Panama. She is author or editor of 20 books, including *Introduction to Community Development* and *Community Development Indicators*

Measuring Systems. She is editor for the *Community Quality of Life and Well-Being* series with Springer, is President of the International Society of Quality-of-Life Studies, http://www.isqols.org, and is a Fellow of the American Institute of Certified Planners (FAICP).

Contributors

Hynsun Choi is Professor in the Department of Public Administration at Myong-Ji University. He researches and teaches community development, social capital, urban policy, and planning. Dr. Choi received his Ph.D. and MPDS from University of Southern California, and M.A. and B.A. in Public Administration from Yonsei University, Seoul, Korea.

Yunji Kim is a doctoral student in the Department of City and Regional Planning at Cornell University. She received her master's degree from the Graduate School of Public Administration, Seoul National University. Her current research interests include the relationship between community well-being and local government services; citizen participation; and community development.

Sharan Merriam is Professor Emeritus of Adult Education and Qualitative Research at The University of Georgia in Athens, GA, USA. Merriam's research and writing activities have focused on adult and life-long learning and qualitative research methods. For five years she was coeditor of *Adult Education Quarterly*, the major research and theory journal in adult education. She has published 27 books and over 100 journal articles and book chapters. She is a four-time winner of the prestigious Cyril O. Houle World Award for Literature in Adult Education for books published in 1982, 1997, 1999, and 2007. Her most recent books are *Adult Learning: Linking Theory and Practice* (2014), *The Jossey-Bass Reader on Contemporary Issues in Adult Education* (2011), *Qualitative Research: A Guide to Design and Implementation* (2016), *Third Update on Adult Learning Theory* (2008), *Learning in Adulthood* (2007), and *Non-Western Perspectives on Learning and Knowing* (2007). She has been a Fulbright Scholar and a Senior Research Fellow in Malaysia, and a Distinguished Visiting Scholar at universities in South Korea and South Africa.

Chaebong Nam is CeRI postdoctoral Research Fellow at Cornell Law School, and former Research Fellow of the Community Wellbeing Project (September 2013–June 2014), Korea.

David C. Sloane is Professor in the Price School of Public Policy at the University of Southern California. He researches and teaches community health planning, food security, public safety, and commemoration from historical and contemporary perspectives. In collaboration with a criminologist and social psychologist, he has participated in a series of studies starting in the mid-1990s looking at issues of public safety and community well-being in the Los Angeles, California, metropolitan region.

HeeKyung Sung is a faculty associate in the School of Community Resources and Development at Arizona State University. She holds her Ph.D. degree from Arizona State University. Her research interests center on the impacts and values of arts and cultural events on local community, and their relationships with overall community well-being. Her prior experience includes over three years experience with a cultural nonprofit organization, the Seongnam Cultural Foundation in Korea. She holds a bachelor's degree in Music Performance and a master's degree in Music Education from Seoul National University.

Geoffrey Woolcock is Manager, Research & Strategy at Wesley Mission Brisbane and Adjunct Associate Professor, Griffith University's School of Human Services and Social Work; and QUT's School of Public Health and Social Work. Geoff works with a diverse range of public and private sector organisations helping develop whole of community outcome measures for a variety of social interventions, particularly in socio-economically disadvantaged communities. He is an experienced social researcher with considerable expertise in social and community service planning and evaluation, including social impact assessment and project evaluation. He has more than 25 years' community-based research experience nationally and internationally, in housing, youth and health sectors, originally in HIV/AIDS prevention and education, culminating in his Ph.D. thesis on AIDS activism completed in 2000. He is a board director on the Australian National Development Index (ANDI), the Brisbane Housing Company and the Logan Child-Friendly Community Charitable Trust, a critical catalyst for the Logan Together collective impact initiative, for which Geoff chairs its Research Alliance.

Chapter 1
Conceptualizing a Community Well-Being and Theory Construct

HeeKyung Sung and Rhonda Phillips

Abstract This chapter focuses on a comprehensive understanding of the concept of community well-being and develops a construct based on several common characteristics. Building on theoretical approaches, this construct helps explain aspects of community well-being. The basic premise of this paper is that community well-being is a comprehensive concept covering other related life and community aspects. The term community well-being encompasses comprehensive and integrated concepts developed by synthesizing research constructs related to residents' perceptions of the community, residents' needs fulfillment, observable community conditions, and the social and cultural context of the community. Related terms such as well-being, happiness, and quality of life take on crucial roles in constructing community well-being. The construct presented is inspired by well-established theoretical analysis such as systems theory, bottom-up spillover theory, social capital and needs theory. Community well-being is a relatively new idea in social science, in this modern rendition of its applications. It still lacks the theoretical structure to explain or predict, and the exploration of related theoretical basis is important for fostering understanding of its application and structure. This chapter strives to help develop a construct for promoting further understanding.

Keywords Quality of life · Community well-being · Theory · Happiness · Community development

From the ancient Greek Philosopher Aristotle to Bentham to present scholars, a significant body of research concerning well-being has been developed in various academic fields. In this context, an understanding of community well-being draws upon a wide range of studies such as welfare, quality of life, community

H. Sung (✉)
Arizona State University, Tempe, USA

R. Phillips
Purdue University, West Lafayette, USA
e-mail: rphillips@purdue.edu

© Springer International Publishing Switzerland 2016
Y. Kee et al. (eds.), *Social Factors and Community Well-Being*,
SpringerBriefs in Well-Being and Quality of Life Research,
DOI 10.1007/978-3-319-29942-6_1

1

satisfaction, community development, sustainability, and personal well-being (e.g. life satisfaction, and happiness) (Assche et al. 2010; Christakopoulou et al. 2001; Forjaz et al. 2011; Keyes 1998; Maybery et al. 2009; Sirgy et al. 2000, 2010; Sirgy and Cornwell 2001; Theodori 2001; White 2010; Wills 2001). Since one universal definition is lacking, these words are used interchangeably in academia and in practice, even though parts of the concepts and disciplines differ widely.

This chapter focuses on a comprehensive understanding of the concept of community well-being and developing a construct based on several common characteristics evident in the literature. The basic premise of the study is that community well-being is a comprehensive concept covering other related life and community aspects. For example, if a community reaches a status of well-being, it can be assume that, to an extent, people are satisfied with living in the community, and the community offers certain standards with respect to both infrastructure and community systems. Also, community well-being is significantly driven by residents' quality of life or their happiness. In addition, potential data gauging community well-being emanates not only from peoples' perceived feeling and evaluation of their life circumstances, but also objective indices such as crime, poverty, and voter rate. To reach a comprehensive concept of community well-being, we discuss the various concepts and elements related to community well-being. By integrating these components, a construct of community well-being is presented, consisting of four major community domains - human, economic, social, and environmental. Further, this construct is driven by three well-established theoretical bases: systems theory, bottom-up spillover theory, and needs theory.

What is community well-being? The term encompasses comprehensive and integrated concepts developed by synthesizing research constructs related to residents' perceptions of the community, residents' needs fulfillment, observable community conditions, and the social and cultural context of the community. Using community well-being as an umbrella concept, related terms such as well-being, happiness, quality of life and community development take on crucial roles in constructing community well-being. As the basis of well-being in the community, these common characteristics are related to each other. Subsequently, since community well-being is a relatively new idea in social science, it still lacks the theoretical structure for explanatory purposes. Finding and understanding the theoretical basis is important. Next, four relevant concepts related to community are discussed—well-being, happiness, quality of life, and community development. Following this discussion, we present three theoretical approaches relevant to community well-being.

Related and Relevant Concepts

Well-being. From hedonic and positive psychology perspectives, well-being indicates how well a person's life is going. Prilleltensky and Prilleltensky (2012) emphasize that relational and collective dynamics of well-being consist of five components:

site, signs, sources, strategies and synergy. On the other hand, Seligman (2012) structures well-being theory into five elements: positive emotion, engagement, relationships, meaning and achievement. He argues that, "the way we choose our course in life is to maximize all five of these elements" (p. 25) and that these elements contribute to well-being as a whole. Diener (2000) focuses on subjective well-being, which refers to peoples' cognitive and affective evaluations of their lives. Defining a good life requires evaluating subjective well-being, and it is connected to a subjective quality of life. He also suggests that well-being results from components of subjective well-being such as life satisfaction, satisfaction with important domains, positive affect, and low levels of negative affect. However, even though he posits a subjective viewpoint of well-being, he agrees that cultural and social factors influence subjective well-being as well (Diener 2000). It might be hard for individuals to change their level of well-being without environmental changes, and vice versa. Well-being has to embrace not only an individual's pleasure, enjoyment, and satisfaction but also the environmental conditions under which people live; we see it as germane to community well-being.

Happiness. Defining *happiness* might be a meaningless endeavor since each person reflects on it differently. Happiness consists in a person's overall emotional condition such as affective states, mood and propensities. Haybron (2008) introduces pleasure, life satisfaction and emotional state as a nature of happiness. Also, Seligman (2012) mentions that happiness is one measurement of life satisfaction and composed of entirely subjective matters. On the other hand, O'Neill (2006) states that the determinants of happiness are relative income, security, worth of work, family relationship, health, freedoms, and social relationship in a community. In other words, happiness can be reflected from the situations people encounter. Further, people who feel good might be more likely to deal with surrounding circumstances positively and favorably. Happiness can be seen as being conducive to building a healthy community and also related to overall community well-being.

Quality of life. The term *quality of life* (QOL) is generally deemed the overall well-being of individuals and societies. The World Health Organization Quality of Life Group (1993) defines QOL as:

> An individual' perception of their position in life in the context of the culture and value systems in which they live … incorporating in a complex way the person's physical health, psychological state, level of independence, social relationships, personal beliefs and their relationship to salient features of the environment (as cited in Rapley 2003, p. 50).

Also, Sirgy and colleagues focus on people's satisfaction from different life domains as a barometer of QOL (Sirgy et al. 2000, 2007, 2010). They advocate that satisfaction with specific and various life events affects satisfaction with each life domain; that affection within life domains accumulates and leads to overall life satisfaction. In this sense, many QOL researchers support subjective characteristics as measurement of QOL. These subjective aspects of QOL are referred to the level of satisfaction that people experience about different dimensions of their lives, the degree of enjoyment of important possibilities in their lives, and individual's perceived well-being (Farquhar 1995; Galambos 1997; Raphael et al. 1997).

On the other hand, Cummins et al. (1997), and Cummins (2000) posit an integration of subjective and objective perspectives in order to construct comprehensive understanding of QOL and develop Comprehensive Quality of Life Scale (ComQol). They define QOL as:

> Both objective and subjective, each axis being the aggregate of seven domains: material well-being, health, productivity, intimacy, safety, place in community, and emotional well-being. Objective domains comprise culturally relevant measures of objective well-being. Subjective domains comprise domain satisfaction weighted by their importance to the individual (Cummins et al. 1997, p. 9).

In a similar manner, Kelley-Gillespie (2009) constructs QOL based on six major life domains such as social, physical, psychological, cognitive, spiritual, and environmental well-being. The Economist Intelligence Unit's QOL index is composed of nine QOL factors: material well-being, health, political stability and security, family life, community life, climate and geography, job security, political freedom, gender equality (Economist Intelligence Unit 2005). Further, Matarrita-Cascante (2010) claims, "QOL is a concept that defines a state of human life situation" (p. 108). He argues that a state refers to a reflection of various conditions such as well-being, welfare, life satisfaction, happiness, poverty, living standards, and development.

There are several common views of QOL studies. QOL embraces "the totality of human life" (Cummins 2000); QOL has multidimensional factors measured by different life domains regardless of an emphasis on either subjective or objective aspects of life; and QOL encompasses various units of society from individual to community, to national, and to global level (Sirgy et al. 2000). Additionally, as a reflection of values that exist in a community (Phillips and Pittman 2009), assessment of QOL is not only germane to residents' well-being, happiness, and satisfaction status quo, but also conducive to building and improving a healthy community which embodies community well-being. Thus, QOL accounts for a large part within a construction of community well-being.

Community Development. This concept is actually far more than conceptual. Community development as a discipline and practice is well established and centers on improving people's conditions in the built, social, environmental, and economic dimensions as communities of place. It can be seen as an ally for promoting community well-being, and also as a complementary framework for understanding and designing research and practice approaches. The theories listed below, along with that of social capital, conflict, symbolic interaction, and communicative action theories are embedded within community development (along with allied disciplines in the social sciences).

Community development is all about capacity building, so that people can accomplish what they need or desire to do within their places. It centers on relationships such as trust, reciprocity, and the ability to organize and mobilize resources. It is both a process and an outcome, and one definition (just as with community well-being, quality of life, and happiness, there are many definitions) is as follows:

A process: developing the ability to act collectively; and an outcome: (1) taking collective action and (2) the result of that action for improvement in a community in any or all realms: physical, environmental, cultural, social, political, economic, etc. (Phillips and Pittman 2015, 8).

The difference between community well-being and community development lies in this process, as the latter is about taking action in the public and social sectors, along with private sector partners to achieve desirable goals. Community well-being on the other hand, is more about gauging what is currently being experienced. The role and intersection of community development in community well-being is one that merits further exploration, to discover relevancy and usefulness in promoting understanding of each, and to develop more effective applications (Lee et al. 2015).

Relevant Theories

Systems theory. This theory aligns very well with the Aristotelian worldview, "the whole is greater than the sum of its part." A system is defined as a set of elements standing in interrelation with environment. As living systems, community is an open system presenting import and export, and building up and breaking down of community components (Von Bertalanffy 1972).

In the context of community well-being, general systems theory highlights the importance of the interaction between people and components of community domains (e.g., human, economic, social and environmental) and between community domains (Kelley-Gillespie 2009). Under a big community well-being marquee we see support by four significant buttresses—human, economic, social, and environmental—and all related concepts such as quality of life, life satisfaction, subjective and objective well-being, and others mingling together. We express this via the four relevant concepts as seen in Fig. 1.1.

Bottom-up spillover theory. Sirgy and colleagues advocate that satisfaction with specific and various life events leads to overall life satisfaction (Choi et al. 2007; Sirgy and Cornwell 2001; Sirgy et al. 2010).

The basic premise of this theory is that overall life satisfaction is functionally related to satisfaction with all of life's domains and subdomains, and in the same way, satisfaction with events and experiences spill over into satisfaction with life's domains. It is usually explained by a satisfaction hierarchy model (see Fig. 1.2).

Bottom-up spillover theory can be adapted for use within community well-being. As a whole, is influenced by community domains (e.g., economic, human, environmental, and social). These domains are composed of sub-domains, and in turn, are affected by specific events or experiences with those domains. Objective and subjective indicators at the bottom of the triangle can be a tool for measurement, as well as a reflection of multi-faceted human needs (see Fig. 1.3). That is, community well-being is constructed from individual concerns with each domain. Consequently, the greater the fulfillment within specific indices, the greater the actualization of community well-being.

Fig. 1.1 Systems of
community well-being

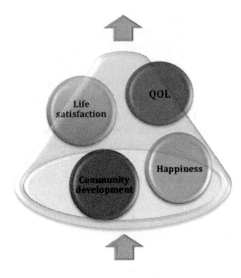

Fig. 1.2 Satisfaction
hierarchy model by Sirgy
et al. (2010)

Fig. 1.3 CWB satisfaction
hierarchy model

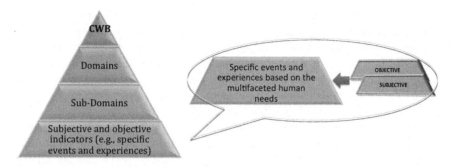

Fig. 1.4 Recognition and evaluation of various human needs in community life by subjective and objective indicators

Needs theory. Needs theory relates to QOL and well-being. 'Needs' derives from research indicating human wants, desires and goals toward well-being and QOL improvement. Humans have certain classes of needs such as freedom needs, welfare needs, and security needs which lead to community consensus and requirement. This theory can be an instrumental in guiding and monitoring potential harmful effects and developing more needs to satisfy and improve well-being (See Fig. 1.4). Nowell and Boyd (2010) regard community as a resource for meeting physiological or psychological needs of humans (Fig. 1.4).

In the context of the community well-being construct, the more human needs are met by community, the more people are likely to experience positive community-well-being. Also, these needs are measured by subjective and objective community indicators which are defined as bits of information, that when combined can paint a picture of what is happening in a community—moving forward, declining, stabilizing, etc. across a variety of factors (Phillips 2003). Indicators should reflect community circumstances; thus, the priorities and sub-measurement items can be variously based on residents' needs, community environment, and their governance (i.e., a distressed community vs. an affluent community).

Conceptualization: Community Well-Being

Although there is not one universal community well-being definition, several definitions have been proposed in the literature. Wiseman and Brasher (2008) define community well-being as "the combination of social, economic, environmental, cultural, and political conditions identified by individuals and their communities as essential for them to flourish and fulfill their potential" (p. 358). McGregor (2007) stresses that well-being arises "in the context of society and social collectivity" (p. 318) and is influenced by social, economic, political, cultural and psychological processes of society. Thus, the concept of community well-being centers around the combination of what a community has, what residents can do with their community assets, and how residents think about community assets and their abilities (McGregor 2007; Murphy 2010). Also emphasized is the importance of not only the objective conditions of community but also residents' subjective perception of their circumstances. In this context, community well-being is regarded as an outcome of community life, and as a state of being that stems from the dynamic interaction of outcomes and processes (McGregor 2007).

In the same vein, Cuthill (2004) approaches community well-being as an outcome of the complex interrelationships between "democratic governance, economic development, environmental sustainability, and social equity and justice" (p. 8). Also, he argues that five key capital assets (i.e., social, human, physical, financial, and natural capital) contribute to the development of community well-being. In this article, Cuthill argues that, "community well-being is the ultimate goal of all democratic governance including that delivered by local government" (p. 9). The focus is more on human and social capital achieved by citizen participation rather than financial, natural, and physical capitals. From the asset-centered approach, understanding community opportunities and constraints is critical for building human and social capital as a basis for community well-being.

In a similar manner, Maybery et al. (2009) approach community well-being as community resilience of residents coping with their stressful circumstances. They regard social connectedness and social ties as critical determinants for community resilience and well-being. The authors, from a survey of small inland rural communities in Australia, demonstrate that these social assets are the most valued in the community as a way to build community well-being. A research study done by Finlay et al. (2010) emphasizes that social factors such as education, employment and working conditions, health care services, housing, social safety, communications, and special factors that depend on community context are important for understanding community wellness. These factors are related to community health outcomes, especially in a distressed community, and enhancements of these factors influence the rebuilding of a community as well.

Further, community well-being identified by the Local Government Community Services Association of Australia (LGCSAA) encompasses "qualities for developing healthy and sustainable communities" (Derrett 2003, p. 53; Wills 2001). For a holistic approach to local community well-being, the concept is grounded in local democracy, active citizenship, cultural community well-being values, a sense of local place and community identity, and social justice and capital (Wills 2001). Wills mentions that community well-being is the state of balancing the demands of environmental sustainability and goals of economic development, and such outcomes (e.g., community livability, sustainability, and vitality) that residents can have from achieving a state of balance. In other words, community well-being here is overall quality of community comprised of social, environmental, human and economic conditions, in balance.

Defining Community Well-Being

Based on the previous discussions, we integrate the various concepts and elements in order to conceptualize community well-being construct. As a result we think community well-being can be defined as:

Community Well-Being (CWB) is a combination of the people and environment;

CWB is not a thing; rather, it is a construct evolved from various community factors;

CWB construct encompasses other life and community related concepts;

CWB is a level of community actualization;

CWB is conceived as multidimensional values including human, economical, social, and environmental factors; and

CWB indicators, both subjective and objective indicators, not only diagnose overall community well-being circumstances, but also help develop future plan to resolve community issues; those indicators can be multifaceted based on the community circumstances.

Development of a Community Well-Being Construct

The construct we present is a combination of deductive and inductive ways of thinking and is driven by three well-established theoretical bases—systems theory, bottom-up spillover theory, and needs theory.

Theories support the conceptualization of the community well-being construct. As seen in Fig 1.5, first general systems theory highlights the importance of the

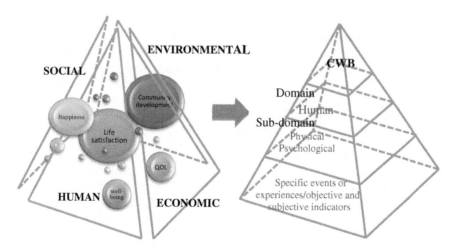

Fig. 1.5 Community well-being construct

interaction between concepts related to people's life and community (e.g., quality of life, life satisfaction, community development, and happiness), as well as four community domains. Within the concept of community well-being, they mingle together and make a comprehensive pool for creating synergy effect.

Second, bottom-up spillover theory explains a hierarchy of community well-being and supports how community well-being can be measured. Community well-being as a whole is influenced by an individual level of concerns through objective and subjective indicators that people develop. Further, it shows an inductive way of approach, while it rests on theoretical validation.

Last, in the context of community well-being construct, needs theory gives a credence letter to bottom-up spillover theory. It claims that a wide range of human needs should be satisfied for human welfare. That is, people are likely to feel community-well-being when a community can help meet their needs. Citizen's needs, community environment, and their governance are reflected in the state of overall community well-being.

Conclusion

While defining community well-being is complicated, this chapter describes a community well-being construct based on four significant community characteristics (human, economics, social, and environmental). First of all, community well-being is inherent in a combination of the people and community environment. Community well-being arises from individual levels of well-being of residents who live in the community. Community well-being can then be considered a critical determinant and consequence of individual well-being, or quality of life. As an umbrella concept, community well-being embraces individual well-being, QOL, and by extension, community development. Further, it includes social norms and values, and various qualities of community.

Second, community well-being is conceived as multidimensional values including economic, social, environmental, and human factors. Even though each domain takes on an important role in the construct of community well-being respectively, there is much variation based on residents' needs, community environment, and their governance structure and effectiveness. It is important to note that the proposed construct should be considered flexible, to reflect multifaceted ways of thinking and gauging well-being.

Acknowledgments This chapter was presented at the 3rd International Forum on Community Well-being on June 23rd, 2015 at the Hoam Faculty House, Seoul, South Korea and was supported by the National Research Foundation of Korea Grant funded by the Korean Government (NRF-2013S1A3A2054622).

References

Assche, J. V., Block, T., & Reynaert, H. (2010). Can community indicators live up to their expectations? The case of the Flemish City monitor for livable and sustainable urban development. *Applied Research Quality Life, 5*, 341–352.

Choi, H., Lee, M., Im, K. S., & Kim, J. (2007). Contribution to quality of life: A new outcome variable for mobile data service. *Journal of the Association for Information Systems, 8*(12), 598–618.

Christakopoulou, S., Dawson, J., & Gari, A. (2001). The community well-being questionnaire: Theoretical context and initial assessment of its reliability and validity. *Social Indicators Research, 56*, 321–351.

Cummins, R. A. (2000). Objective and subjective quality of life: An interactive model. *Social Indicators Research, 52*, 55–72.

Cummins, R. A., McCabe, M. P., Romeo, Y., Reid, S., & Waters, L. (1997). An initial evaluation of the comprehensive quality of life scale: Intellectual disability. *International Journal of Disability, Development and Education, 44*(1), 7–19.

Cuthill, M. (2004). Community well-being: The ultimate goal of democratic governance. *Queensland Planner, 44*(2), 8–11.

Derrett, R. (2003). Making sense of how festivals demonstrate a community's sense of place. *Event Management, 8*, 49–58.

Diener, E. (2000). Sujective well-being: The science of happiness and a proposal for a national index. *American psychologist, 55*(1), 34–43.

Economist Intelligence Unit. (2005). The Economist Intelligence unit's quality-of-life index. Retrieved December 2, 2012, from http://www.economist.com/media/pdf/QUALITY_OF_LIFE.pdf.

Farquhar, M. (1995). Elderly people's definitions of quality of life. *Social Science and Medicine, 41*(10), 1439–1446.

Finlay, J., Hardy, M., Morris, D., & Nagy, A. (2010). Mamow Ki-ken-da-ma-win: A partnership approach to child, youth, family and community well-being. *International Journal of Mental Health Addiction, 8*, 245–257.

Forjaz, M. J., Prieto-Flores, M. E., Ayala, A., Rodriguez-Blazquez, C., Fernandez-Mayoralas, G., Rojo-perez, F., et al. (2011). Measurement properties of the community well-being index in older adults. *Quality Life Research, 20*, 733–743.

Galambos, C. M. (1997). Quality of life for the elder: a reality or an illusion? *Journal of Gerontological Social Work, 27*(3), 27–44.

Haybron, D. M. (2008). *The pursuit of unhappiness: The elusive psychology of well-being.* Oxford, UK: Oxford University Press.

Kelley-Gillespie, N. (2009). An integrated conceptual model of quality of life for older adults based on a synthesis of the literature. *Applied Research Quality Life, 4*, 259–282.

Keyes, C. L. M. (1998). Social well-being. *Social Psychology Quarterly, 61*(2), 121–140.

Lee, S., Kim, Y., & Phillips, R. (2015). Exploring the intersection of community well-being and community development (pp. 1–8). In *Community well-being and community development, conceptions and applications.* SpringerBriefs in Well-Being and Quality of Life Research Series, Dordrecht, The Netherlands: Springer.

Matarrita-Cascante, D. (2010). Changing communities, community satisfaction, and quality of life: A view of Multiple perceived indicators. *Social Indicators Research, 98*, 105–127.

Maybery, D., Pope, R., Hodgins, G., Hitchenor, Y., & Shepherd, A. (2009). Resilience and well-being of small inland communities: Community assets as key determinants. *Rural Soceity, 19*(4), 326–339.

McGregor, J. A. (2007). Research well-being: From concepts to methodology. In I. Gough & J. A. McGregor (Eds.), *Well-being in developing countries: From theory to research* (pp. 316–355). New York: Cambridge University Press.

Murphy, B. (2010). *Community well-being: An overview of the concept.* Toronto, Canada: Nuclear Waste Management Organization.

Nowell, B., & Boyd, N. (2010). Viewing community as responsibility as well as resource: Deconstructing the theoretical roots of psychological sense of community. *Journal of Community Psychology, 38*(7), 828–841.

O'Neill, J. (2006). Citizenship, well-being and sustainability: Epicurus or Aristotle? *Analyse & Kritik, 28,* 158–172.

Phillips, R. (2003). *Community indicators.* Chicago, IL: American Planning Association.

Phillips, R., & Pittman, R. H. (2009). A framework for community and economic development. *An introduction to community development,* 3–19.

Phillips, R., & Pittman, R. (2015). A construct for community and economic development. In R. Phillips & R. H. Pittman (Eds.), *An introduction to community development* (pp. 7–10). London: Routledge.

Prilleltensky, I., & Prilleltensky, O. (2012). Webs of well-being: The interdependence of personal, relational, organizational and community well-being. In J. Haworth & G. Hart (Eds.), *Well-being: individual, community and social perspectives.* New York, NY: Palgrave Macmillan.

Raphael, D., Brown, I., Renwick, R., & Rootman, I. (1997). Quality of life: What are the implications for health promotion? *American Journal of Health and Behavior, 21*(2), 118–128.

Rapley, M. (2003). *Quality of life research: A critical introduction.* Thousand Oaks, CA: SAGE Publications.

Seligman, M. E. P. (2012). *Flourish: A visionary new understanding of happiness and well-being.* New York, NY: Free Press.

Sirgy, M. J., & Cornwell, T. (2001). Further validation of the Sirgy et al.'s measure of community quality of life. *Social Indicators Research, 56,* 125–143.

Sirgy, M. J., Grzeskowiak, S., & Rahtz, Z. (2007). Quality of college life (QCL) of students: Developing and validating a measure of well-being. *Social Indicators Research, 80*(2), 343–360.

Sirgy, M. J., Rahtz, D. R., Cicic, M., & Underwood, R. (2000). A method for assessing residents' satisfaction with community-based services: A quality-of-life perspective. *Social Indicators Research, 49,* 279–316.

Sirgy, M. J., Widgery, R. N., Lee, D., & Yu, G. B. (2010). Developing a measure of community well-being based on perceptions of impact in various life domains. *Social Indicators Research, 96,* 295–311.

Thodori, G. L. (2001). Examining the effects of community satisfaction and attachment on individual well-being. *Rural Sociology, 66*(4), 618–628.

Von Bertalaffy, L. (1972). The history and status of general systems theory. *Academy of Management Journal,* 407–426.

White, S. C. (2010). Analysing well-being: A construct for developing practice. *Development in Practice, 20*(2), 158–172.

Wills, J. (2001). Measuring community well being: A construct for the development of community indicators. In *Local Government Community Services Association of Australia (LGCSAA) 8th Biennial National Conference,* Perth, Australia.

Wiseman, J., & Brasher, K. (2008). Community well-being in an unwell world: Trends, challenges, and possibilities. *Journal of Public Health Policy, 29,* 353–366.

Chapter 2
Structure of Well-Being: An Exploratory Study of the Distinction Between Individual Well-Being and Community Well-Being and the Importance of Intersubjective Community Well-Being

Seung Jong Lee and Yunji Kim

Abstract Despite the popularity of well-being in public policy discourses, the meaning of well-being and how to use it in a public policy context is still unclear. In this chapter, we present a comprehensive framework of well-being that clarifies its meaning by distinguishing different types and aspects of well-being. First, we distinguish individual well-being and community well-being. Since public policy concerns public resources, we further explore the aspects of community well-being. Previous works only identified objective and subjective aspects of community well-being, leading to confusion in the measurement process regarding aggregation from individuals to the community. To address this issue, we identify a third aspect called intersubjective community well-being measured by evaluative questions. Using survey data from six districts in Seoul, South Korea, we show that individual well-being and community well-being can be distinguished empirically and that the relationship between intersubjective and objective community well-being is stronger than the relationship between subjective and objective community well-being. This suggests that policymakers can gain better insight for policymaking by paying more attention to intersubjective community well-being, which effectively bridges relevant objective measures to collective evaluation of citizens.

Keywords Community well-being · Intersubjective community well-being · Community resources · Public policy

S.J. Lee (✉)
Seoul National University, Seoul, South Korea

Y. Kim
Cornell University, Ithaca, USA

© Springer International Publishing Switzerland 2016
Y. Kee et al. (eds.), *Social Factors and Community Well-Being*,
SpringerBriefs in Well-Being and Quality of Life Research,
DOI 10.1007/978-3-319-29942-6_2

Introduction

In recent years, ideas of well-being, quality of life, and happiness have become popular in the public policy world. Australia, Canada, France, Germany, Italy, South Korea, and the UK are some countries that have either already incorporated or plan to incorporate these ideas into public policy. These concepts are often placed in juxtaposition to gross domestic product (GDP), inequitable economic growth, and narrow definitions of progress (i.e. accumulation of wealth) to describe alternative visions of society. However, their meanings are still ambiguous and it is unclear how these concepts relate to broader public policies since they have mostly been studied in a select few fields in academia, such as economics, health, and psychology. This confusion has led to voices of criticism and caution against using these words in public policy (see Booth 2012; Scott 2012). Nevertheless, the GDP framework that narrowly focuses on economics has limitations as a vision of social progress. The recent interest in well-being can be seen as evidence of a demand for a more comprehensive framework. However, in order for well-being to serve as a viable alternative, scholars must clarify the concept with both theory and empirical data.

Well-being has been used interchangeably with quality of life and happiness in the past, but we exclusively focus on well-being as it is a more comprehensive term that can serve as an umbrella concept (Lee and Kim 2015). However, well-being is still misconstrued and thus fails to provide helpful directions for public policy decisions. We present a well-being framework that clarifies its structure to address this limitation. In particular, we focus on two limitations in previous works. First, previous attempts to use well-being in public policy have not adequately distinguished individual well-being (IWB) from community well-being (CWB). This has led to a mismatch of using measurements of an individualistic concept (i.e. IWB) in a discussion about the use and distribution of public resources. Second, the measurement of CWB has been limited to objective and subjective aspects, failing to capture the collective characteristic of CWB. This limitation arises when we try to measure something about the collective (i.e. CWB) but we need to resort to gathering information from the individual members of the collective. The objective aspect does not reflect any input from the actual community members, while the subjective aspect can become too individualistic. We introduce intersubjective CWB as a third aspect that can resolve these issues.

In exploring the structure of well-being, we first explain why CWB measurement is necessary given the long history of quality of life (QOL) indicators and community indicators. We discuss the limitations of previous indicators and how CWB indicators can address them. Next, we address more specific concerns with using well-being and its indicators in public policy discourses and present a new framework of well-being. Our framework distinguishes IWB from CWB and identifies three aspects of CWB. Previous understandings of CWB have mainly focused on its objective and subjective aspects (McCrea et al. 2006; Schneider 1975; Veenhoven 2002), neglecting the intersubjective CWB. This third aspect is important for creating measures of a community level concept with data collected from individuals without letting the individualistic characteristic overshadow the collective characteristic.

Finally, we test our framework using survey data from Seoul, South Korea. We find that CWB and IWB can be empirically distinguished. As such, CWB is a concept that should be studied as distinct from IWB and one that is more appropriate for discussions of public policy. We also find that while previous works have focused on measuring subjective CWB through satisfaction questions, the relationship between intersubjective CWB (measured by evaluative questions) and objective CWB (i.e. community resources) is stronger than that between subjective CWB and objective CWB. We argue that intersubjective CWB is an area that needs more future study.

Limits of Previous Indicators

In this section, we review the limitations of QOL indicators and community indicators. This is to set the stage for Part III where we propose a new well-being framework to address these limitations. While QOL indicators and community indicators may not use the exact term "community well-being," they share the general purpose of assessing how well a group is doing and to improve conditions for a larger group. In fact, many have treated these terms synonymously in the past (Bunge 1975; McMahon 2002; Swain and Hollar 2003). While we agree that there are overlapping parts among these terms, we also show that there are differences among them and argue that CWB measures can give a more complete picture than QOL measures or community indicators.

Scholars identify the early 1960s with the birth of the social indicators movement when NASA and the American Academy of Arts tried to measure the impact of the space race on American society. This was an effort spearheaded by the government to gather information about society that GDP was unable to capture. QOL indicators grew out of this larger social indicators movement, but with a more explicit focus on quality, rather than quantity. Many QOL indicator projects have been launched by national governments and public policy institutes since the 1970s, but they have mostly been limited to western countries as can be seen in the literature. For example, the *Handbook of Social Indicators and Quality of Life Research* edited by Land et al. (2012) is comprised of chapters on North American and European cases with a few chapters that explicitly deal with select countries in East Asia and Latin America. While this may be indicative of a western bias, it also accurately reflects the strong roots of the QOL movement in the western world.

An implication of the QOL movement's roots in the western world is the lack of a collective conception. In other words, the QOL concept is strongly individualistic with its ultimate focus on the well-being of individuals, and largely belongs to the realm of psychologists (Sawicki 2002). In addition to psychology, the QOL concept has been extensively studied in the health and medicine disciplines. The use of QOL concept in public health dates back to the 1940s when the World Health Organization embraced this concept in its constitution (WHO 1948). During the 1990s and 2000s, scholars developed measures of QOL related to various medical conditions (Patrick and Chiang 2000; Stewart and Ware 1992).

Accordingly, we see serious limitations to using QOL in a public policy context. First, an individualistic approach like QOL can conflict with public values that should heavily influence decisions about the use and allocation of public resources. Not only can individual preferences conflict with each other, but also what is beneficial to each individual can lead to negative outcomes for the entire group. For example, automobiles increase mobility for individuals, reducing travel time and increasing comfort. However, if too many individuals opt for this travel mode, roads can quickly become congested and decrease benefits for the entire group. An individualistic concept has serious limitations for guiding public policy.

Second, since much of the research on QOL comes from the field of psychology, health, and medicine there may be limitations of generalizability for a general public policy framework. Works that relate to certain diseases or disabilities tend to focus on a problem or deficiency that can be identified. Public policy also tries to diagnose social problems and cure them, but it goes beyond simply solving problems to making things better. The findings from the field of medicine and health are unable to take us beyond solving issues. Another limitation is the lack of a public policy framework from the research on QOL in these fields. The solutions that are proposed in these studies rarely require a collective group's approval, but tend to be a private discussion between patients, their families, and doctors that ultimately lead to a private decision. In contrast, public policy decisions usually go through a complex process that involves many actors. Few QOL indexes distinguish input, throughput, and output (Hagerty et al. 2001), offering little direction for public policy.

Community indicators can solve some of these limitations. First, community indicators take the community as its unit of analysis, rather than individuals. There is some variation in the definition of community indicators. For example, some define it as "measurements of local trends that include all three dimensions of what it takes to build a healthy community—economic, environmental, and social" (Smolko 2006, p. 1) while others have defined it as "sets of data used to measure the progress of an area over time" (Philips and Bridges 2005, p. 115). Nevertheless, most community indicators focus on the collective group.

Despite this improvement from QOL indicators, community indicators still paint an incomplete picture because they are heavily focused on objective measures. For example, Kim and Lee (2013) reviewed fifty three community measurement projects and found that despite efforts to include both objective and subjective measurements, there are still more objective indicators than subjective. This focus on objective data is not surprising, given the community indicators movement's connection to community development theories that emphasize community capitals (Flora and Flora 2013) and assets (Green and Haines 2007). However, objective indicators provide an incomplete picture as they lack any input from the community, such as preferences (Veenhoven 2002). Cobb and Rixford (2005) pointed out that community indicators have successfully described the status of communities, but have offered little in terms of prescription. We argue that even as a descriptive tool, community indicators are limited because an assessment of the amount of community capital and assets does not necessarily give an accurate measurement of the level of CWB, or whether the needs of the community are being adequately addressed. For example, a community might be rich in capitals and assets, but if they are only accessible to a select few, we can hardly say that this community has high levels of CWB.

In sum, QOL and community indicators have mainly two limitations. First, QOL indicators are mainly focused on the individual and are unable to provide an accurate assessment of CWB. While a community is certainly a collection of individuals, it is also more than the simple sum of individuals. IWB can give some indication of the level of CWB, but they are not identical. On a practical level, local governments can take note of subjective well-being, happiness, or life satisfaction levels of individuals to assess the presence of problems, but these indicators do not give direction to what areas the local government can or should focus on improving. Second, community indicators mostly offer objective information and lack subjective information. We acknowledge that objective conditions and resources are important ingredients of CWB, but equally important is the community's assessment of these resources and how they are being used. Therefore, we call for the adoption of a framework that gives adequate attention to the community level and contains both objective and subjective measurements.

A New Framework of Well-Being

Few scholars are against measuring well-being altogether, but there have been disagreement about whether this information should be used for policy decisions and especially about the danger of ignoring power dynamics and politics involved in this process. In other words, critics are concerned with the cooptation of the term "well-being" to advance a select group's agenda or interest at the cost of others'. White (2010) identifies four hazards of well-being, and while her work is focused on developing countries in particular, these hazards have also been cause for concern in the broader well-being literature. The four hazards are as follows: (1) well-being might be conceived as something that is important only after the basic human needs are met (2) a focus on well-being as a strictly emotional assessment might lead to the conclusion that state aid or welfare is not important since people in places with weak social safety nets can also have a high life satisfaction score (3) well-being is an inherently liberal and individualistic concept that emphasizes self-help and can lead to blaming individuals for their conditions or the way they feel (4) well-being as a holistic concept can be too broad and be of little use in policy analysis.

In this section, we present a well-being framework that addresses these major concerns. We are certainly not the first or only scholars to address these concerns. Sirgy et al. (2010) proposed a CWB measure based on the bottom-up spillover theory of life satisfaction. They recognized the limitations of previous indicators that only ask broad questions about satisfaction with community, which fail to provide detailed diagnostic and prescriptive information. Their measure of CWB covers the following fourteen life domains: safety, social, leisure, family and home, political, spiritual, neighborhood, environmental, transportation, education, health, work, financial, and consumer. However, these measures are still focused on satisfaction levels only and do not address the concern that a well-being focus might ignore objective needs.

We explicitly address the four hazards of well-being summarized by White (2010). First, our framework includes both objective and subjective aspects, addressing the first hazard. Second, we introduce the intersubjective CWB component to give CWB a richer meaning than mere emotions. Third, we argue that public policy should give more weight to CWB rather than IWB. And lastly, we tried to define CWB and identify the types of CWB to make this concept clearer.

Figure 1 is a visual illustration of our proposed well-being framework. The horizontal and vertical axes were chosen to highlight the limitations in previous indicators. The vertical axis shows the unit of analysis—individual or community—while the horizontal axis shows the objective or subjective aspect of the concepts. We argue here that IWB and CWB are distinct concepts. The former focuses on an individual's resources that can be treated as private property and an individual's perception of his or her life. The latter is about public or communal resources and how well the community needs are met. In the lower half of the figure that deals with IWB, we identify an objective IWB and subjective IWB; the former refers to the individual resources while the latter is an individual's perception of them. Another way to understand the objective and subjective distinction is to see objective aspects as inputs in a policy process and subjective aspects as outputs. In the upper half of the figure that deals with CWB, we also identify an objective CWB and subjective CWB, but unlike IWB we identify a third type of CWB called intersubjective CWB. We use the concept of intersubjective CWB due to complexities in collective well-being that we discuss in detail below.

Previously, we defined CWB as a concept about meeting the needs and desires of a community (Lee and Kim 2015). This definition was derived from previous definitions of CWB and IWB. While both concepts share at its core the idea of well-being, the point of departure can be found in the process of aggregation. We begin with a discussion of IWB as it is relatively less complex, compared to CWB.

Objective IWB has been measured with indicators such as income, education, life expectancy, depression, and presence of chronic illness. We note that these indicators have also been referred to as social indicators, but we call them objective IWB indicators because they are ultimately about the individual; aspects of life that an individual has substantial levels of control over and for which society assumes significant levels of individual responsibility. Subjective IWB has been measured by happiness and life satisfaction (also known as subjective well-being

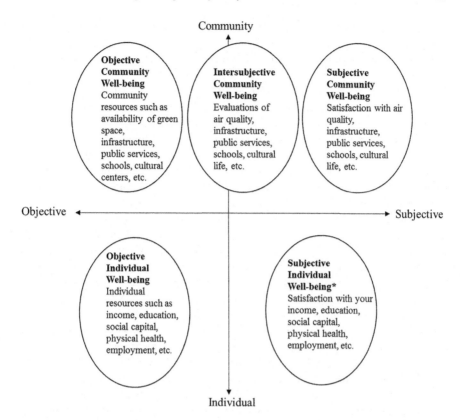

Fig. 2.1 Proposed Framework of Well-being (also known as subjective well-being (SWB) in previous literature)

or SWB in the happiness and psychology literature). Regarding the relationship between objective IWB and subjective IWB (i.e. the lower half of Fig. 2.1) while there is some evidence to the contrary (e.g. Easterlin Paradox, Hedonic Treadmill Theory), empirical research largely suggests a significant and positive relationship between the two domains (Blanchflower and Oswald 2004; Di Tella et al. 2003; Inglehart 1990).

We now return to the problem of aggregation in CWB. Objective CWB is fairly straightforward; these could be measured by levels of community resources, such as public space or public services. However, when we consider theories of community that argue a collective is more than the sum of its individuals (Durkheim and Lukes 2014; Gherardi and Nicolini 2000), there is no omniscient collective being whom we can ask about the level of subjective CWB. An extension of this confusion arises in the relationship between objective and subjective CWB. While there is a relatively more direct relationship between objective IWB elements and subjective IWB elements, this is not true for CWB elements. The relationship between community resources and collective satisfaction is difficult to test and even after testing it, the exact process of how community resources (e.g. local government services or public expenditure) affect communal satisfaction is elusive. This is our reasoning for proposing a third type of CWB called intersubjective CWB.

Intersubjectivity was first defined by philosopher Edmund Husserl at the beginning of the 20th century. The term has been used in European and American social science fields since the 1960s and is commonly defined as the knowledge that is shared between two or more conscious minds or shared understanding. However, scholars have pointed out that this common definition is one that is detached from Husserl's original writings and is much narrower than the original concept (Duranti 2010; Quincey 1999; Rogoff 1990; Tomasello and Carpenter 2007; Trevarthen and Hubley 1978). Based on a close reading of Husserl's work, Duranti (2010) argues that intersubjectivity is more than shared or mutual understanding, but rather about the possibility of "trading places." He explains that the narrow definition of intersubjectivity fails to explain empathy. When we feel empathy for another person we do not necessarily read another person's mind or come to the same understanding about the world, but instead think about the possibility of seeing the world from someone else's perspective. The concept is fundamentally about relationships between and among individuals. Thus this idea is useful when discussing collective levels of well-being. The concept allows us to move away from the previously individualistic nature of well-being measures.

We use an example to illustrate the three different types of CWB. For example, I may be dissatisfied with the level of traffic in my district, but at the same time I can be aware that the reason there is congestion in my district is because it is a desirable place to live. This is a relatively more objective way of thinking, because I can recognize the congestion as a given community parameter. At the same time, I can recognize that in comparison to other districts, my district is making adequate efforts for dealing with traffic congestion by placing police officers to direct traffic during rush hour. My satisfaction with the traffic situation can be different from my evaluation of it. We call the former (i.e. satisfaction) subjective CWB and the latter (i.e. evaluation) intersubjective CWB.

Intersubjective CWB is particularly useful for discussions about public resources. We want public resources to both efficiently and adequately meet community needs and demands. For example, the number of public libraries in a district can be high, which would show up as high objective CWB scores, but what we really want is for the resources to adequately match the need of communities. If there is relatively less need for public libraries, then this means there may be waste of public resources and while people might be satisfied with the services, it is not the most efficient use of public resources.

Another advantage of measuring intersubjective CWB is it allows for a more collective mindset and thus a more accurate reflection of CWB, rather than the simple aggregation of IWB. In a district with low levels of public services for the elderly, someone can be very satisfied with these levels of public services because he or she has enough personal resources to access these services through private means (e.g. private nursing homes), but he or she can still think with a more communal framework that the level of public service for the elderly in this district is inadequate. This mental exercise of "trading places" with another person is in line with the more robust definition of intersubjectivity that Duranti (2010) emphasized.

In summary, previous works on well-being measurement have focused on the IWB quadrants (i.e. lower two quadrants of Fig. 2.1). In comparison, there has been less effort to look at the upper half of Fig. 2.1 and especially the area between objective CWB and subjective CWB. All areas in Fig. 2.1 are important and necessary in their own right, but scholars of public policy and planning should at least pay equal attention, if not more, to the collective part of the well-being framework. In detail, we argue there needs to be clarification of the CWB concept as distinct from IWB and the relationships among objective, subjective, and intersubjective CWB. We use survey data to address these needs.

Methodology

The purpose of our study is to test empirically whether IWB and CWB can be distinguished and discover the relationship between objective CWB (i.e. community resources), subjective CWB (i.e. satisfaction), and intersubjective CWB (i.e. evaluation). While there have been extensive research on IWB, there has been relatively little work on CWB and our work is largely exploratory. We use structural equation modeling to test our proposed well-being framework and one-way ANOVA and correlation analysis to examine the relationships among objective, subjective, and intersubjective CWB.

The Community Well-Being Survey

Our research questions require information on various types of well-being: objective CWB, subjective CWB, intersubjective CWB, subjective IWB, and objective IWB. While objective community indicators (e.g. number of libraries, number of schools, etc.) are available through the Korean Statistical Information Service website (KOSIS; www.kosis.kr), there is little information on intersubjective CWB and subjective CWB; mostly limited to one item surveys that ask about happiness or overall satisfaction with the community. Thus, we designed and administered the Community Well-being Survey with the Community Well-being Institute in the following six local districts in Seoul, South Korea: Dongdaemun gu (population 363,258), Gangnam gu (population 564,197), Guro gu (population 427,520), Jongno gu (population 165,207), Jung gu (population 133,360), and Mapo gu (population 384,644). These six districts were chosen to increase the representativeness of our sample with small districts and large districts within Seoul. Local governments in Korea are organized in a two tier system: metropolitan level and local level. As of 2013, Korea had 17 metropolitan governments that are further divided into 227 local si (74), gun (84), gu (69) units. In 2012, the total non-foreigner population of Seoul Metropolitan City was approximately 10.2 million with the average local government district (gu) population of approximately 408,000.[1] The Seoul metropolitan city is divided into 25 gu districts. The Survey used convenience sampling of adults age 20 or older who reside in these districts. All data were collected from January 2013 to February 2013 via self-administered questionnaires.

The questionnaire was broadly divided into four parts that ask questions about both IWB and CWB in the following format: close-ended questions on community and individual satisfaction, close-ended questions on community evaluation, open-ended questions on CWB, and demographic information (e.g. household income, education level, employment status, marital status). This study mainly uses responses from the first two parts on IWB and CWB. Questions in the first part asked for personal satisfaction levels that pertain to individual life and community life on a 10 point Likert scale (subjective IWB and subjective CWB), while questions in the second part asked respondents to evaluate the level of various aspects of community life on a 10 point Likert scale (intersubjective CWB). Demographic variables, which were used as indicators of objective IWB, were also close-ended questions. Household income and education questions asked respondents to choose among 13 categories and 5 categories, respectively (see Table 2.1). Employment and marital status were re-coded as dummy variables to have value of one for currently employed and currently married status, and then summed to create an employment and marital status parcel.

Analysis

This paper has two main goals: (1) to determine the measurement model of well-being (2) to describe the relationship between objective CWB, subjective CWB, and intersubjective CWB. We use a structural equation modeling for the first goal as we wish to build a theory of CWB structure—a topic that has relatively little previous findings—and a one-way ANOVA and correlation analysis for the second goal.

We first checked for missing data in raw file (3.6 %), which showed that household income and questions on evaluation of community economic items were most often missing. Household income, in particular, shows a strong left skew with most of the responses clustered around the higher income ranges. Little's MCAR test showed that data were not missing completely at random; therefore, we used the expectation maximization (EM) method for imputation. Our final sample size after EM imputation was 900 with more female respondents (59 %) than males (41 %). In terms of age, our sample has most respondents in their 30s (25 %), 40s (22 %), and 20s (20 %).

---

[1] All population figures are based on the national resident registry data.

Table 2.1 Sample characteristics

Variable	Category	Frequency (%)
Gender	Female	59
	Male	41
Age	20–29	20
	30–39	25
	40–49	22
	50–59	17
	60–69	10
	70–79	5
	80 and above	0.3
Household income[a]	Less than 500 thousand KRW	3
	500 thousand–990 thousand KRW	3
	1.00 million–1.49 million KRW	6
	1.50 million–1.99 million KRW	7
	2.00 million–2.49 million KRW	9
	2.50 million–2.99 million KRW	9
	3.00 million–3.49 million KRW	13
	3.50 million–3.99 million KRW	8
	4.00 million–4.49 million KRW	9
	4.50 million–4.99 million KRW	7
	5.00 million–5.49 million KRW	8
	5.50 million–5.99 million KRW	4
	6.00 million KRW and more	16
Education[a]	Less than elementary school	2
	Middle school	4
	High school	23
	University	58
	Graduate school or higher	13
Employment[a]	Dummy, 1 = Currently employed	63
Marital status [a]	Dummy, 1 = Currently married	66

Source 2013 Community Well-being Survey
Note: N = 900. 1019 KRW is approximately equal to 1 USD. Percentages may not add to 100 due to rounding
[a]Used as indicator of objective IWB

Since the survey was focused on CWB we had far more variables pertaining to subjective CWB (27) and intersubjective CWB (29) than subjective IWB (5) and objective IWB (4). For model convergence purposes and reliability, we created composite average indexes (or parcels) for subjective and intersubjective CWB variables. Appendix 1 shows the questionnaire items that were used to create the composite variables of CWB.

We hypothesized four possible measurement models using our survey data on subjective CWB, intersubjective CWB, subjective IWB, and objective CWB.

First, a two factor model that only distinguishes IWB related items from CWB related items. Second, a three factor model that further differentiates IWB into subjective and objective, but still considers the CWB related items to load on one factor. Third, another three factor model that differentiates intersubjective CWB from subjective CWB, but sees IWB items as loading on one general IWB factor. Fourth, a four factor model that differentiates intersubjective CWB, subjective CWB, subjective IWB, and objective IWB. We also tested an alternative two factor model that only differentiates data into subjective and objective factors to include all empirically possible measurement models. Following Kline's (2011) advice on testing measurement models in areas with little theory on the number of factors, we first evaluated a single factor model wherein all items load on a general well-being factor. The parsimony principle would suggest that given similar fit to the same data a simpler model is preferred. Thus if we cannot reject the simple one factor model, there is weak support to model more complex ones.

According to Kline (2011), a rule of thumb for extreme skewness or kurtosis is absolute values of skew index (SI) above 3 and absolute values of kurtosis index (KI) above 10. Most variables in our structural equation modeling analysis show approximate univariate normal distribution. However, a test of multivariate normality suggested severe skewness (41.38 SI = 49.25) and kurtosis (633.54 KI: 35.815), and thus we used a robust maximum likelihood method of estimation. All latent variables were scaled using unit loading identification for disturbances of endogenous variables. All analyses were performed with LISREL 8.80. Table 2.2 shows descriptive statistics for all model variables.

We report the following model fit statistics: model chi-square, Steiger-Lind root mean square error of approximation (RMSEA; Steiger 1990) with its 90 % confidence interval, Bentler Comparative Fit Index (CFI; Bentler 1990), and adjusted goodness of fit index (AGFI). The model chi-square tests the exact fit hypothesis and thus a significant p-value leads us to reject our hypothesized model. A limitation of the model chi-square statistic is its sensitivity to sample size; in large samples even small discrepancies between the hypothesized model and data can result in a statistically significant model chi-square. Kline (2011) reports that for typical sample sizes in structural equation modeling (between N = 200 and 300) this is less likely. Our sample size (N = 900) is much larger than this and it is highly likely that we will see significant model chi-square values that would ordinarily lead us to reject the hypothesized model. However, we report these numbers because they will be the basic statistic for comparing alternative measurement models. For RMSEA, we follow Browne and Cudeck's (1993) suggestion of values less than or equal to 0.05 as indicating "close fit" and values between 0.05 and 0.08 as "adequate fit." Accordingly, the lower boundary of the 90 % confidence interval should be less than 0.05 while the upper boundary should be less than 0.10. For CFI and AGFI, higher values indicate better fit with CFI values greater than 0.97 indicating "good fit" and values above 0.90 for AGFI (Schermelleh-Engel et al. 2003).

It is important to keep in mind that our purpose in this study is slightly different from the usual goal of structural equation modeling. We do not wish to

Table 2.2 Descriptive statistics of continuous variables (N = 900)

Latent variable	Manifest variable	Mean	SD	Min	Max	Skew-ness (SI)	Kurtosis (KI)	Cronbach's alpha
Subjective (satisfaction) CWB	Public works/ infrastructure	6.34	1.50	1.2	10	−0.03 (−0.39)	−0.21 (−0.71)	0.85
	Environment	5.48	1.86	1.0	10	0.10 (1.28)	−0.14 (−1.38)	0.75
	Social	5.75	1.52	1.3	10	0.19 (2.29)	−0.15 (−0.89)	0.94
	Local public administration	5.81	1.72	1.0	10	0.03 (0.38)	−0.11 (−0.66)	0.93
	Safety	5.81	1.65	1.0	10	0.00 (0.02)	0.07 (0.52)	0.88
	Economy	5.44	1.47	1.0	10	0.13 (1.59)	0.18 (1.08)	0.90
Intersubjective (evaluation) CWB	Public works/ infrastructure	6.11	1.54	1.0	10	0.01 (0.13)	−0.15 (−0.95)	0.91
	Environment	5.46	1.85	1.0	10	0.11 (1.35)	−0.21 (−1.34)	0.79
	Social	5.68	1.52	1.0	10	0.22 (2.72)	0.04 (0.31)	0.96
	Local public administration	5.76	1.72	1.0	10	0.03 (0.38)	0.09 (0.62)	0.95
	Safety	5.75	1.68	1.0	10	0.09 (1.13)	−0.08 (−0.45)	0.91
	Economy	5.55	1.50	1.0	10	0.13 (2.55)	0.18 (1.00)	0.93

(continued)

Table 2.2 (continued)

Latent variable	Manifest variable	Mean	SD	Min	Max	Skew-ness (SI)	Kurtosis (KI)	Cronbach's alpha
Subjective IWB	Health	6.38	1.76	1.0	10	−0.19 (−2.27)	0.06 (0.45)	N/A[a]
	Culture and arts activity	6.10	2.00	1.0	10	−0.12 (−1.51)	−0.36 (−2.61)	
	Social/community life	5.69	1.72	1.0	10	0.16 (1.96)	0.35 (1.94)	
	Volunteer	5.54	1.79	1.0	10	0.28 (3.33)	0.19 (1.16)	
	Job	5.77	1.89	1.0	10	−0.03 (−0.35)	0.03 (0.26)	
Objective IWB	Household income	7.88	3.47	1	13	−0.04 (−0.48)	−1.01 (−14.29)	
	Education	3.77	0.79	1	5	−0.90 (−9.61)	1.61 (5.90)	
	Employment and marital status	1.29	0.66	0	2	−0.39 (−4.65)	−0.76 (−7.78)	

Source 2013 Community Well-being Survey
[a]N/A = not applicable

model causal relationships among latent variables, but rather to see how many latent variables can be measured in our data. Thus we evaluate several hypothetical measurement models and compare them using the model chi-square statistic.

Based on the results of our measurement models, we then move on to our second task of examining relationships between objective CWB, subjective CWB, and intersubjective CWB. Since the CWB Survey does not have objective CWB measures, we used the Seoul Survey data available through the KOSIS website. Our objective CWB scores were calculated as follows. We gathered various community indicators of the six districts from the Seoul Survey available through the KOSIS website that roughly correspond to the CWB variables in our survey. Some examples are the number of hospitals, area of green space, number of childcare centers, local government budget on education, number of 911 fire/emergency centers, local financial autonomy, etc. (see Appendix 2 for complete list of indicators). We converted all indicators to a z-score and then created a summative score for each district. We examined Pearson correlations among objective CWB, subjective CWB, and intersubjective CWB. Lastly, because we wanted know more about intersubjective CWB—an aspect of CWB that has previously been ignored—a one-way ANOVA analysis was used to test the null hypothesis that all districts have equal mean scores of intersubjective CWB. Next, we used a post hoc analysis of mean differences to compare the differences in intersubjective CWB scores across districts.

Results

Types of Well-Being

Since the parsimony principle dictates that given a similar model fit, a simpler model is better, we first tested a one factor model wherein all items load on a general well-being factor. The one factor model fit indexes generally did not indicate good fit with chi-square value of 2024.581 (df = 170, $p = 0.0$), RMSEA = 0.110 (0.106; 0.114), AGFI = 0.686, except CFI = 0.958.

Therefore, we proceeded with the more complex two factor model of CWB and IWB. The model fit indices for this model showed little change from the one factor model with RMSEA = 0.110 (0.105; 0.114), AGFI = 0.687, and CFI = 0.958. Still, the model chi-square value decreased to 1999.068 (df = 169), and a chi-square difference test (Δchi-square = 23.787, Δdf = 1) indicated that this is a statistically significant improvement to the original one factor model (see Table 2.3). Thus, our results show that CWB can be measured as a distinct concept from IWB and raise questions on previous community indicator systems that treated IWB and CWB to be identical or regarded CWB as simply the sum of IWB.

We also evaluated an alternate two factor model that distinguishes all subjective well-being items from objective well-being items. However, we did not find evidence that this model is statistically better than the original one factor model.

Table 2.3 Model Fit Statistics

Model	RMSEA	RMSEA 90 % C.I.	CFI	AGFI	χ^{2a} (df)	p	χ^2 difference test[b] (Δdf)	Model Comparisons
One factor measurement model	0.110	0.106; 0.114	0.958	0.686	2024.581 (170)	0.0		
Two factor measurement model 1 (subjective CWB and IWB)	0.110	0.105; 0.114	0.958	0.687	1999.068 (169)	0.0	23.787*** (1)	Two factor measurement model 1 compared to one factor measurement model
Two factor measurement model 1 (subjective well-being and objective well-being)	0.111	0.106; 0.115	0.958	0.684	2024.361 (169)	0.0	0.200 (1)	Two factor measurement model 2 compared to one factor measurement model
Three factor measurement model 1 (subjective CWB, subjective IWB, objective IWB)	0.110	0.105; 0.114	0.959	0.686	1968.722 (167)	0.0	30.354*** (2)	Three factor measurement model 1 compared to two factor measurement model 1
Four factor measurement model (evaluation subjective CWB, satisfaction subjective CWB, objective IWB subjective IWB)[c]	0.108	0.103; 0.112	0.961	0.696	1870.593 (164)	0.0	58.426*** (3)	Four factor measurement model compared to three factor measurement model 1

***$P < 0.01$

Note We evaluated the three factor measurement model 2 (subjective CWB, intersubjective CWB, IWB) but the solution was not admissible after 50 iterations

[a]Satorra Bentler Scaled chi square

[b]The chi square difference statistic can be used to compare the overall model fit of two hierarchical or nested models by examining the simple difference in chi square statistic and degrees of freedom. However, we cannot use corrected model chi squares, such as the Satorra Bentler Scaled chi square, to perform such chi square difference tests as the difference between corrected model chi squares do not follow a chi square distribution. Instead, we use the following Satorra-Bentler corrected chi-square difference test (TRd) as defined in Satorra and Bentler (2001)

$$TRd = T0-T1/Cd, Cd = (r0c0-r1c1)/(r0-r1)$$

where

T0: chi-square value of nested model M0

r0: degrees of freedom of nested model M0

c0: scaling correction factor for model M0, calculated as T0/Satorra Bentler corrected T0

T1: chi-square value of nested model M1

r1: degrees of freedom of nested model M1

c1: scaling correction factor for model M1, calculated as T1/Satorra Bentler corrected T1

[c]The covariance matrix of independent variables were not positive definite in this four factor model. We report the fit indices for reference only

This may be seen as further support for our argument that mixing IWB with CWB is inappropriate. The model fit indices of RMSEA (0.111), CFI (0.958), and AGFI (0.684) were nearly identical to the one factor model, and the model chi-square difference test (Δchi-square = 0.200, Δdf = 1) failed to show that this is a statistically significant change.

Although the two factor measurement model of CWB and IWB was an improvement from the one factor measurement model, the model fit indices still suggested poor fit. As such, we proceeded to test the more complex three factor models. We hypothesized two possible three factor models: one in which only IWB is further separated into subjective and objective and an alternative in which only CWB is further separated into subjective (measured by satisfaction questions) and intersubjective (measured by evaluation questions). The first model with CWB, subjective IWB, and objective IWB shows little change in fit indices compared to the two factor model (CWB and IWB), which is our best model so far. The model fit indices are as follows: model chi-square = 1968.722 (df = 167), RMSEA = 0.110 (0.105; 0.114), CFI = 0.959; AGFI = 0.686, indicating poor fit with the exception of CFI. The model chi-square difference test (Δchi-square = 30.354, Δdf = 2) shows that this three factor model has better fit than the two factor model.

The alternate three factor model with CWB further divided to subjective CWB (i.e. satisfaction) and intersubjective CWB (i.e. evaluation) did not lead to an admissible solution after 50 iterations. An inspection of the covariance matrix of factors suggests that subjective CWB and intersubjective CWB may have high collinearity and thus it does not seem likely that we will find better fit with more complicated models.

We tested our last hypothetical measurement model of four factors and while the software LISREL did not issue a message for inadmissible solution, the covariance matrix of independent variables were not positive definite. We report the fit indices for this model in Table 2.3 for reference only. This indicates that intersubjective and subjective CWB have low discriminant validity in our data. However, we keep intersubjective CWB and subjective CWB as separate variables since our second goal is to examine how these are related to objective CWB.

Three Aspects of Community Well-Being: Objective, Subjective, and Intersubjective

Our ultimate goal is to connect the aspects of CWB measured through a survey— subjective CWB and intersubjective CWB—to objective CWB for public policy decisions. Objective CWB, which is what community indicator projects have mostly focused on, is an important element for this goal because governments can have substantive control over these public resources. The composite z-score of objective CWB varied among the six districts even though they are within the same metropolitan city of Seoul and they were ranked as follows: Gangnam gu (9.79), Jung gu (6.73), Jongno gu (6.67), Mapo gu (−2.23), Guro gu (−11.10), Dongdaemun gu (−11.61).

Table 2.4 Pearson correlations for CWB variables

	Objective CWB	Intersubjective (evaluation) CWB
Intersubjective (Evaluation) CWB	0.777* $p = 0.069$	
Subjective (Satisfaction) CWB	0.716 $p = 0.109$	0.987*** $p = 0.000$

$*p < 0.1$, $**p < 0.05$, $***p < 0.01$

First, we used a Pearson's product-moment correlation to assess the relationship between objective CWB scores and the following variables: intersubjective (evaluation) CWB and subjective (satisfaction) CWB. We used scatter plots to check linear relationships and all variables were approximately normally distributed, and there were no extreme outliers. There was a strong positive correlation between objective CWB and intersubjective and subjective CWB (see Table 2.4). The correlation between intersubjective CWB and objective CWB (0.777, $p = 0.069$) was stronger than that between subjective CWB and objective CWB (0.716, $p = 0.109$). Our results from the structural equation modeling analysis indicated that subjective and intersubjective CWB are difficult to distinguish. However, our correlation analysis shows that subjective and intersubjective CWB have a different relationship with objective CWB; the relationship between intersubjective CWB and objective CWB is slightly stronger and statistically significant ($p = 0.010$) while the relationship between subjective CWB and objective CWB is not.

Intersubjective CWB scores were distributed the following way, from highest to lowest: Gangnam gu (M = 37.77, SD = 8.72), Mapo gu (M = 35.80, SD = 8.17), Jongno gu (M = 35.68, SD = 7.71), Jung gu (M = 33.20, SD = 7.21), Dongdaemun gu (M = 32.19, SD = 9.29), Guro gu (M = 30.19, SD = 6.92). Figure 2.2 is a visual representation of the mean intersubjective CWB score for each district, with the numbers below the district name showing its ranking in objective CWB scores for comparison. For example, Gangnam gu had the highest score of intersubjective CWB score, and also objective CWB score, while Mapo gu had the second highest intersubjective CWB score, but ranked fourth on the objective CWB score. Levene's Test of Homogeneity of Variance ($p = 0.001$) indicated that the assumption of homogeneity of variances was violated and we report appropriate modified statistics. We found that intersubjective CWB scores were statistically significantly different between different districts, Welch's F (5, 353.04) = 20.28, $p = 0.000$.

While places with high objective CWB scores tend to have higher intersubjective CWB scores, their rankings were not identical. For example, Mapo gu ranked fourth on objective CWB scores, but second on intersubjective CWB scores. In other words, Mapo gu may not have a lot of community resources as compared to the other five districts, but their evaluation of the Mapo district was higher in comparison to other districts with higher objective CWB. This may indicate that

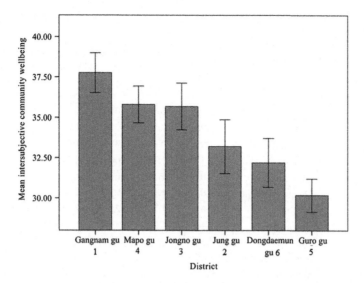

Fig. 2.2 Mean Intersubjective CWB Scores by District. *Source* Authors' calculations. *Note* Numbers under the district name represent ranking of objective CWB scores. For example, "*1*" represents highest objective CWB score. Error bar shows 95 % confidence interval

increasing intersubjective CWB may require a more careful assessment of community needs and demands than simply increasing community resources.

We also conducted a Games-Howell post hoc analysis to further examine which districts differ on intersubjective CWB and by how much. Table 2.5 shows the comprehensive results with the base district in the order of objective CWB ranking, from highest to lowest. In other words, we look at Gangnam gu as the first base district for comparison since it has the highest objective CWB score, and then Jung gu (second highest), Jongno gu and so on. The largest mean differences are between Gangnam gu and Guro gu, Mapo gu and Guro gu, Gangnam gu and Dongdaemun gu, and Jongno gu and Guro gu, in order of decreasing mean difference. There was a statistically significant decrease in intersubjective CWB score from Gangnam gu, the district with highest objective CWB score to Guro gu, Dongdaemun gu, and Jung gu. The largest mean decrease was between Gangnam gu and Guro gu, a mean decrease of 7.58, 95 % CI [5.10, 10.07], which was statistically significant ($p = 0.000$). Comparison between the second highest ranking objective CWB district, Jung gu, and other districts with lower objective CWB scores are less pronounced and none of them were statistically significant. The mean difference between Jongno gu and Guro gu were significant with mean decrease of 5.50, 95 % CI [2.62, 8.37]. Jongno gu and Dongdaemu gu also showed a statistically significant difference in mean score of 3.49, 95 % CI [0.49, 6.48]. Mapo gu showed a statistically significant difference in mean scores with both Guro gu and Dongdaemun gu, with values of 5.62, 95 % CI [3.15, 8.09] and 3.61, 95 % CI [1.02, 6.20], respectively.

Table 2.5 Games-Howell Post Hoc Analysis Results of District Mean Differences in Intersubjective CWB

District with higher objective CWB score (I)	District with lower objective CWB score (J)	Mean difference (I − J)	Std. error	Sig.	95 % confidence Interval	
					Lower bound	Upper bound
Gangnam gu	Guro gu	7.58*	0.85	0.000	5.10	10.07
	Dongdaemun gu	5.57*	0.89	0.000	2.97	8.18
	Mapo gu	1.96	0.82	0.228	−0.45	4.37
	Jongno gu	2.09	0.97	0.366	−0.73	4.90
	Jung gu	4.57*	1.11	0.000	1.39	7.74
Jung gu	Guro gu	3.016	1.13	0.091	−0.22	6.25
	Dongdaemun gu	1.01	1.16	0.999	−2.35	4.36
	Mapo gu	−2.61	1.11	0.211	−5.76	0.55
	Jongno gu	−2.48	1.22	0.468	−6.05	1.08
Jongno gu	Guro gu	5.50*	0.99	0.000	2.62	8.37
	Dongdaemun gu	3.49*	1.02	0.010	0.49	6.48
	Mapo gu	−0.12	0.96	1.000	−2.92	2.67
Mapo gu	Guro gu	5.62*	0.84	0.000	3.15	8.09
	Dongdaemun gu	3.61*	0.88	0.001	1.02	6.20
Guro gu	Dongdaemun gu	−2.01	0.91	0.336	−4.67	0.65

$*p < 0.05$

Conclusion

Previous attempts to include well-being in public policy discussions have been less than successful because of the ambiguity and confusion around the concept. In this chapter, we presented a framework of well-being to clarify its structure and used empirical data to test this framework. In detail, previous works have failed to appreciate the distinction between CWB and IWB, and ignored the intersubjective aspect of CWB. Our framework distinguishes CWB from IWB and identifies three aspects of CWB: subjective, objective, and intersubjective. Based on survey data from Seoul, South Korea we found that CWB and IWB can be empirically distinguished and that intersubjective CWB, rather than subjective CWB, is closely related to objective CWB. We summarize our key findings below.

Previous approaches that fail to distinguish IWB and CWB lead to confusion when we try to use the well-being concept in public policy decisions. IWB is largely within the private realm that governments have little control over. Thus mistaking IWB scores for CWB scores can lead to frustration when governments see that there is little improvement. Confusing IWB with CWB can also lead citizens to blame governments when they do not see a clear improvement in IWB levels when in fact, governments have little control over the elements of IWB. A proper measure of CWB is important for connecting well-being to government.

The hypothesized distinction between subjective CWB scores and intersubjective CWB scores was not supported by our data. Even so, we argue that intersubjectivity is an important type of CWB to measure based on our correlation analysis results. Objective CWB is a measure of community resources that the local government has considerable control over. We found that the relationship between intersubjective CWB and objective CWB is distinct from and stronger than that between subjective CWB and objective CWB. Theoretically, the use of intersubjective scores as a measure of how well community resources are meeting community needs and desires may be more appropriate than subjective scores because they allow a more objective and public-minded assessment of community conditions. Practically, this suggests a possibility for using intersubjective CWB scores when there is little or no information on objective CWB.

The relationship between intersubjective CWB and objective CWB is an area that needs more future research. This is the link that can effectively connect well-being and public policy decisions, and our results show that the relationship may not be straightforward. For example, Mapo gu district ranked fourth on objective CWB scores but ranked second on intersubjective CWB scores. Without further research we can only speculate the reason. One possibility is the role of sense of community and social capital. The Mapo gu district is home to an artist community called the Sungmisan neighborhood that is well-known for the strong social ties among its residents (Kee et al. 2013).

This is the first attempt to empirically distinguish IWB and CWB and to examine how intersubjective CWB and objective CWB are related. Our data is limited to a sample of six districts in Seoul, South Korea and thus we need to be cautious about generalizing our results to other communities. Nevertheless, our generic framework of well-being could be tested in other countries. Most importantly, our framework provides a structure of well-being that can be used in a public policy context. If governments' recent interest in well-being is to bring real, positive changes to communities, CWB should be studied in depth as a distinct concept and more information on intersubjective CWB should be collected.

Appendix 1

Questionnaire Items Used for CWB Indicators

	Intersubjective CWB (question format: how would you evaluate…)	Subjective CWB (question format: how satisfied are you with…)
Public works/ infrastructure	Medical service Waste collection Public transportation Internet service Roads	Medical service Waste collection Public transportation Internet service Roads
Environment	Air quality Green space	Air quality Green space

	Intersubjective CWB (question format: how would you evaluate…)	Subjective CWB (question format: how satisfied are you with…)
Social	Culture and art activity level Culture and art activity support Public library Lifelong education Learning environment Services for elderly Services for disabled Childcare services General social services Community activity Volunteer	Culture and art activity level Culture and art activity support Public library Lifelong education Learning environment Services for elderly Services for disabled Childcare services General social services
Local public administration	Local government employee fairness Local government employee attitude/service Overall local government services	Local government employee fairness Local government employee attitude/service Overall local government services
Safety	Natural disaster preparedness Public safety Police	Natural disaster preparedness Public safety Police
Economy	Local government budget size Local government budget management Local taxes Overall economic environment Cost of living	Local government budget size Local government budget management Local taxes Overall economic environment Cost of living

Appendix 2

Indicators Used for Objective Community Well-being Score

Number of medical buildings per capita; number of waste collection trucks per ton of daily waste; number of sanitation worker per ton of daily waste; fine dust ($\mu g/m^3$); nitrogen dioxide, carbon monoxide, sulfurous acid gas emission total (ppm); green space availability per capita; percent household with personal computer; percent households with high-speed internet connection; number of arts and cultural center per capita; number of library per capita; number of lifelong education facilities per capita; lifelong education programs per capita; number of *hagwon* (private tutoring centers) per capita; college entrance rate; education budget per school age population; number of centers for the elderly per population over 65; number of centers for disabled persons, number of childcare centers, index of public employee honest; number of civil petitions processed; population per 911 fire/emergency center[2]; percent of population with training experience in fire situations; percent of population with CPR/First Aid training; percent population registered as community volunteer; local revenue per capita; local financial autonomy rate.

---

[2]Subtracted from total objective CWB score.

Appendix 3

Covariance Matrix Used for Structural Equation Modeling Analysis

	1	2	3	4	5	6	7	8	9	10	11	12	13	14	15	16	17	18	19	20
Health SIWB	3.094																			
Culture SIWB	1.107	3.998																		
Social SIWB	0.951	1.845	2.943																	
Volunteer SIWB	1.007	1.677	2.375	3.161																
Job SIWB	1.050	1.546	1.355	1.307	3.562															
Household income	0.242	0.164	0.056	0.006	0.308	0.631														
Education	0.857	0.606	0.199	0.138	1.240	0.887	12.010													
Employment-marital status	1.239	1.879	1.441	1.394	1.278	0.122	0.620	2.244												
Public works SCWB	1.139	1.502	1.483	1.419	1.221	0.030	0.390	1.650	3.463											
Environment SCWB	1.009	2.209	1.772	1.729	1.575	0.114	0.518	1.700	1.670	2.306										
Social SCWB	1.098	1.588	1.650	1.579	1.543	0.085	0.485	1.565	1.580	1.805	2.956									
Public administration SCWB	1.097	1.851	1.878	1.745	1.633	0.171	0.606	1.712	1.639	1.895	1.991	2.731								
Safety SCWB	1.062	1.765	1.500	1.499	1.441	0.171	0.714	1.922	1.459	1.697	1.629	1.789	2.365							
Economy SCWB	1.045	1.666	1.536	1.570	1.441	0.106	0.620	1.607	2.649	1.728	1.635	1.733	1.864	3.410						
Public works ISCWB	1.054	1.906	1.747	1.774	1.599	0.155	0.609	1.628	1.598	1.972	1.725	1.877	1.974	1.939	2.296					
Environment ISCWB	1.138	1.663	1.700	1.695	1.597	0.107	0.327	1.603	1.534	1.761	2.494	1.933	1.887	1.829	2.034	2.946				
Social ISCWB	1.143	1.822	1.706	1.721	1.612	0.149	0.649	1.704	1.621	1.797	1.871	2.255	2.018	1.893	2.143	2.254	2.832			
Public administration ISCWB	1.085	1.452	1.516	1.480	1.693	0.226	0.897	1.411	1.412	1.566	1.653	1.661	1.580	1.621	1.697	1.742	1.697	2.172		
Safety ISCWB	1.012	1.415	1.336	1.314	1.455	0.226	0.903	1.320	1.344	1.478	1.489	1.563	1.641	1.691	1.775	1.778	1.843	1.766	2.263	
Economy ISCWB	0.016	0.013	0.071	0.032	0.199	0.089	0.313	-.001	0.106	0.052	0.051	0.087	-.008	0.077	0.040	0.039	0.075	0.109	0.091	0.435

Note: *SIWB* = subjective IWB, *SCWB* = subjective CWB, *ISCWB* = intersubjective CWB

Acknowledgments   This chapter was presented at the 3rd International Forum on Community Well-being on June 23rd, 2015 at Hoam Faculty House, Seoul, South Korea and was supported by the National Research Foundation of Korea Grant funded by the Korean Government (NRF-2013S1A3A2054622).

References

Bentler, P. M. (1990). Comparative fit indexes in structural models. *Psychological Bulletin, 107*(2), 238–246.

Blanchflower, D. G., & Oswald, A. J. (2004). Money, sex and happiness: An empirical study. *The Scandinavian Journal of Economics, 106*(3), 393–415.

Booth, P. (Ed.). (2012). *... and the pursuit of happiness-well-being and the role of government.* London: The Institute of Economic Affairs.

Browne, M. W., Cudeck, R., & Bollen, K. A. (1993). Alternative ways of assessing model fit. *Sage Focus Editions, 154*, 136.

Bunge, M. (1975). What is a quality of life indicator? *Social Indicators Research, 2*(1), 65–79.

Cobb, C., & Rixford, C. (2005). Historical background of community indicators. In R. Phillips (Ed.), *Community indicators measuring systems* (pp. 33–62). Burlington, VT: Ashgate.

Di Tella, R., MacCulloch, R. J., & Oswald, A. J. (2003). The macroeconomics of happiness. *Review of Economics and Statistics, 85*(4), 809–827.

Duranti, A. (2010). Husserl, intersubjectivity and anthropology. *Anthropological Theory, 10*(1–2), 16–35.

Durkheim, E., & Lukes, S. (2014). *The rules of sociological method: And selected texts on sociology and its method.* New York, NY: Free Press.

Flora, C. B., & Flora, J. L. (2013). *Rural communities: legacy and change.* Boulder, CO: Westview Press.

Gherardi, S., & Nicolini, D. (2000). The organizational learning of safety in communities of practice. *Journal of Management Inquiry, 9*(1), 7–18.

Green, G. P., & Haines, A. (2007). *Asset building and community development.* Thousand Oaks, CA: Sage.

Hagerty, M. R., Cummins, R. A., Ferriss, A. L., Land, K., Michalos, A. C., Peterson, M., & Vogel, J. (2001). Quality of life indexes for national policy: Review and agenda for research. *Social Indicators Research, 55*(1), 1–96.

Inglehart, R. (1990). *Culture shift in advanced industrial society.* Princeton, NJ: Princeton University Press.

Kee, Y., Kim, S., Kim, N. (2013). Analysis of the community well-being paradigm model Sungmisan village: using grounded theory method of Strauss and Corbin. *Korean Public Administration Review, 47*(1), 295–320. (Korean).

Kim, Y., & Lee, S. (2013). The Development and Application of a Community Well-being Index in Korean Metropolitan Cities. *Social Indicators Research,* 1–26.

Kline, R. B. (2011). *Principles and practice of structural equation modeling* (3rd ed.). New York, NY: Guilford Publications.

KOSIS. (2013). *Seoul survey* [data]. Retrieved from http://kosis.kr/statisticsList/statisticsList_02List.jsp?vwcd=MT_ATITLE01&parmTabId=M_02_01_01

Land, K. C., Michalos, A. C., & Sirgy, J. M. (Eds.). (2012). *Handbook of social indicators and quality of life research.* Dordrecht: Springer.

Lee, S., & Kim, Y. (2015). Searching for the meaning of community well-being. In S. J. Lee, Y. Kim, & R. Phillips (Eds.), *Community well-being and community development: Conceptions and applications.* Dordrecht: Springer.

McCrea, R., Shyy, T.-K., & Stimson, R. (2006). What is the strength of the link between objective and subjective indicators of urban quality of life? *Applied Research in Quality of Life, 1*(1), 79–96.

McMahon, S. (2002). The development of quality of life indicators—A case study from the City of Bristol. *UK. Ecological Indicators, 2*(1), 177–185.

Patrick, D. L. & Chiang, Y. P. (2000). Measurement of health outcomes in treatment effectiveness evaluations: Conceptual and methodological challenges. *Medical Care, 38*(9 Suppl), II14–II25.

Phillips, R., & Bridges, S. (2005). Integrating community indicators with economic development planning. In R. Phillips (Ed.), *Community indicators measuring systems* (pp. 115–138). Burlington, VT: Ashgate Publishing Company.

Quincey, C. (1999). Intersubjectivity: Exploring consciousness from the second-person perspective. In S. R. Hameroff, A. W. Kaszniak, & D. J. Chalmers (Eds.), *Toward a science of consciousness III: The third Tucson discussions and debates*. Cambridge, MA: The MIT Press.

Rogoff, B. (1990). *Apprenticeship in thinking: Cognitive development in social context*. New York, NY: Oxford University Press.

Satorra, A., & Bentler, P. M. (2001). A scaled difference chi-square test statistic for moment structure analysis. *Psychometrika, 66*(4), 507–514.

Sawicki, D. S. (2002). Improving community indicator systems: Injecting more social science into the folk movement. *Planning Theory & Practice, 3*(1), 13–32.

Schermelleh-Engel, K., Moosbrugger, H., & Müller, H. (2003). Evaluating the fit of structural equation models: Tests of significance and descriptive goodness-of-fit measures. *Methods of Psychological Research, 8*(2), 23–74.

Schneider, M. (1975). The quality of life in large American cities: Objective and subjective social indicators. *Social Indicators Research, 1*(4), 495–509. doi:10.1007/BF00353066.

Scott, K. (2012). *Measuring well-being: Towards sustainability?*. New York, NY: Earthscan from Routledge.

Sirgy, M. J., Widgery, R. N., Lee, D.-J., & Grace, B. Y. (2010). Developing a measure of community well-being based on perceptions of impact in various life domains. *Social Indicators Research, 96*(2), 295–311.

Smolko, R. (2006). *The community indicators handbook: measuring progress toward healthy sustainable communities* (2nd ed.). Oakland, CA: Redefining Progress.

Steiger, J. H. (1990). Structural model evaluation and modification: An interval estimation approach. *Multivariate Behavioral Research, 25*(2), 173–180.

Stewart, A. L., & Ware, J. E. (Eds.). (1992). *Measuring functioning and well-being: The medical outcomes study approach*. Durham: Duke University Press.

Swain, D., & Hollar, D. (2003). Measuring progress: Community indicators and the quality of life. *International Journal of Public Administration, 26*(7), 789–814.

Trevarthen, C., & Hubley, P. (1978). Secondary intersubjectivity: Confidence, confiding and acts of meaning in the first year. In A. Lock (Ed.), *Action, gesture and symbol: The emergence of language* (pp. 183–229). London: Academic Press.

Tomasello, M., & Carpenter, M. (2007). Shared intentionality. *Developmental science, 10*(1), 121–125.

Veenhoven, R. (2002). Why social policy needs subjective indicators. *Social Indicators Research, 58*(1–3), 33–46. doi:10.1023/A:1015723614574.

White, S. C. (2010). Analysing well-being: A framework for development practice. *Development in Practice, 20*(2), 158–172.

WHO. (1948). *Constitution of the World Health Organization. Basic documents*. Geneva: World Health Organization.

Chapter 3
Does Sense of Community Matter in Community Well-Being?

Youngwha Kee and Chaebong Nam

Abstract This paper compares one vibrant grassroots community with its surrounding municipality in relation to subjective community well-being. Nested in Mapo munic-ipality, Sungmisan is a small community formed from active community organizing and strong grassroots civic networks. Sungmisan has similar objective conditions—in terms of local public services, or, objective community well-being—to those of Mapo. Still, survey results show that Sungmisan residents were more satisfied with the local public services available in their community than were the Mapo residents with theirs, suggesting that objective community well-being does not always determine subjective community well-being. Community-level characteristics, such as sense of community, appear to be the most likely differentiating influence. Although *sense of community* was not established as a significant variable for subjective community well-being for Sungmisan, Sungmisan displayed high community-oriented characteristics, which was strikingly different from those of Mapo.

Community well-being is gaining ground as a new framework that explains qual-ity of life and happiness in a communal context, rather than on an individual level. Emerging as an important research topic, its measurement typically consists of two aspects: objective data and subjective data (Kim and Lee 2013). Objective data at large represent an external state of well-being, such as conditions of education, public transportation, green spaces, and more in local areas. Subjective data rate residents' perceptions of the community environment as whole or individual indicators of com-munity well-being. In this paper, objective data are defined as *objective well-being*, and subjective data are referred to as *subjective well-being*.

It is generally stated that objective well-being is the key determining factor of subjective well-being. However, the so-called Easterlin paradox shows that

Y. Kee (✉)
Soongsil University, Seoul, Korea
e-mail: youngwhakee@naver.com

C. Nam
Cornell Law School, New York, USA

© Springer International Publishing Switzerland 2016
Y. Kee et al. (eds.), *Social Factors and Community Well-Being*,
SpringerBriefs in Well-Being and Quality of Life Research,
DOI 10.1007/978-3-319-29942-6_3

the relationship is not always secure. Those with better objective well-being—in Easterlin's case, higher income—tend to be happier than those who are poor. Nonetheless, above a certain level of per capita average income, such a positive relationship between objective well-being (income) and subjective well-being disappears (Easterlin 1995). Easterlin's paradox constitutes an important premise of community well-being research that examines various contextual components of community well-being beyond economic factors. In alignment with this issue, we emphasize that perceptions of community well-being (subjective community well-being) are not solely determined by an external state (objective community well-being), but can be influenced by subjective factors as well, particularly by a sense of community.

To this end, we compared a small community known as Sungmisan to the rest of the local municipality where it is nested, in Mapo. Because Sungmisan is part of Mapo, it was assumed that Sungmisan residents experience the same conditions of public services provided by the Mapo local government. Given this state of local services in both areas, the major issues of concern in this paper are whether any differences exist in sense of community and perceptions of community well-being among residents between the two areas, and if so, what influence sense of community has on perceptions of community well-being.

This study is based on survey data completed by approximately 330 residents from Sungmisan and Mapo and is comprised of four sections: the first focuses on the literature regarding the role of sense of community in well-being research; the second describes the methodology including contexts of Sungmisan and Mapo; the third details the results of the analyses; and the fourth provides a discussion of the results.

Sense of Community and Well-being

Sense of community is among the most often studied topics in community psychology, since Sarason (1974) defined sense of community as "the sense that one was part of a readily supportive network of relationships upon which one could depend" (p. 1). Gusfield (1975) indicated two core elements that constitute community: one is a geographical location with which people are identified, and the other is a relational term including social ties, relationships, and networks. Among commonly cited definitions of sense of community is one suggested by McMillian and Chavis (1986) in which four dimensions of sense of community were proposed: membership, influence, integration and fulfillment of needs, and shared emotional connection. Accordingly, McMillian and Chavis defined sense of community as "a feeling that members have of belonging, a feeling that members matter to one another and to the group, and a shared faith that members' needs will be met through their commitment to be together" (p. 9).

In addition to community psychology, sense of community has been discussed as an important research topic in other disciplines including urban planning, geography, environmental psychology, community development, communications, and anthropology. However, different names such as *sense of place*, *place identity*, and *place attachment* are used. Each discipline defines its concepts slightly differently and abides by its own academic traditions, preferred research methods, and issues of interest. Still, common ground exists across the disparities, in which *place* is regarded as a social construct. Place is not simply an object existing apart from human lives that is created upon shared experiences, narratives, and cultural practice (Benson and Jackson 2013; Cornelio and Ardévol 2011; de Certeau 1984; Jorgensen and Stedman 2001; Leander and McKim 2003; Pink 2008; Pierce et al. 2011; Shamai and Ilatov 2005). In this, place is constituted through a wider range of "shared" and multisensorial lived and collaborative productions among people who exchange signs, experiences, and sociocultural practices. This perspective of place is lined up with that of sense of community.

Nonetheless, research about the relationship between sense of community and well-being has chiefly been conducted in community psychology and related fields, and thereby we narrow our scope to community psychology. Sense of community has been considered a critical component of quality of life in local places. A body of literature has discussed the positive relationship between sense of community and personal well-being (or life satisfaction). The relationship between the two is more intuitive than unpredictable, drawing attention from relatively few empirical studies, including Davidson and Cotter (1986). To pursue more sophisticated modeling, several researchers who studied community well-being considered other variables that are presumably associated with sense of community: community variables (characteristics, size, population density of neighborhoods/community, and more); demographic variables (gender, age, marital status, income, level of education, number of children and more); and other variables (owning one's home, number of years lived in the community, community involvement, and more).

Fried (1984) studied how community satisfaction has differing levels of influence on life satisfaction (close to the notion of community well-being) depending on individual socioeconomic status. Local interpersonal satisfaction is one of the four elements of community satisfaction and corresponds to sense of neighborhoods and community. It appeared to contribute to life satisfaction on a very small scale for the lower social class and the high-middle social class. Nevertheless, community satisfaction overall had the highest positive influence on life satisfaction for the lower social class, but the smallest positive influence on the upper social class.

Prezza and Costantini (1998) showed the differing effect of territorial size on sense of community and its relation to life satisfaction. Residents in towns reported a greater sense of community and life satisfaction, and sense of community is positively related to personal well-being only in a small town, and to a lesser degree, in a small city. No significant link between sense of community and life satisfaction was found in larger cities. In a study that followed, however, sense of community was found to have a significant association with life satisfaction and loneliness in all three areas: large towns, small towns, and cities (Prezza et al. 2001).

Farrell et al. (2004) examined the role of sense of community in mediating the relationship between "neighborhood characteristics" and "frequency of neighboring behavior" with personal well-being. The neighborhood characteristics were defined by marital status and mobility (representing "rootedness" or stability). Those with high stability (married and with lower levels of mobility) were related to more neighborliness and a greater sense of community. The positive contribution of sense of community to personal well-being was consistent with results of prior research. In particular, what is notable in the study was the focus on smaller homogeneous neighborhoods as units for analysis, instead of large areas at the census track level that includes heterogeneous neighborhoods.

Mak et al. (2009) investigated sense of community in Hong Kong regarding its relationships with community-level characteristics and resident well-being. In this study, sense of community was positively associated with personal well-being, but not with both individual (gender, age, family income, and the like) and community indicators (population density, stability). The absence of a link between community indicators and sense of community was presumably attributed to Hong Kong's social context—coexistence of heterogeneous neighborhoods in a single district. High heterogeneity may decrease not only neighboring behavior, but also sense of community in a district or a "unit of analysis" using Farrell et al.'s (2004) terminology.

Hombrados-Mendieta et al. (2013) revealed differing influences of sense of community on life satisfaction between immigrants and natives. In the case of a high sense of community, no significant differences were detected between the groups in life satisfaction. In the case of a low or medium sense of community, natives displayed higher life satisfaction than did immigrants, which implies that the negative effect of the migration, a low sense of community, accounts for dwindled life satisfaction in immigrants.

In short, positive associations between sense of community and personal well-being have been repeatedly reported. To obtain a sophisticated understanding of mediating influences of sense of community on life satisfaction, researchers in the aforementioned studies have taken into account community variables such as territorial size, population density, median family income, mobility, and immigration, in addition to individual variables.

Consideration of community variables is also practiced in community well-being research, which emphasizes a holistic approach in addressing the concept of well-being (Cox et al. 2010; Cummins et al. 2003; Cuthill 2002; Hooghe and Vanhoutte 2011; Sirgy et al. 2010; Swain and Hollar 2003). Community well-being research concentrates on communal aspects that are critical for determining quality of life, including local public services and the social and natural environment, rather than individual variables like income and education. Specifically, our concern is how sense of community, a community-level variable, is associated with perceptions of community well-being shared among residents. Given that the two areas are under the same external state of local public services, we investigated the following:

1. What differences are there, if any, in the perceptions of 34 individual community well-being indicators among residents between Sungmisan and Mapo?
2. What differences are there, if any, in sense of community among residents between the two areas?
3. If number 2 is positive, how would the sense of community variable have differing influences on satisfaction with local living conditions and subjective community well-being between the two areas that are located in the same municipality but present contrasting characteristics (size, population density, history) with each other?

Methods

Data were drawn from a survey that included 34 individual community well-being indicators, in addition to questions about demographic information and sense of community. About 200 people from Mapo and 130 people from Sungmisan participated in the survey.

Measurement

Socio-demographic characteristics. Measures of age, gender, marital status, employment status, education, income, years lived in the community, number of children in the household, and more were included. Age, education, and income were measured through an ordinal variable on a scale of 1 through 7 (age and income) and 1 through 5 (education).

For age, 1 means between 20 and 29, 2 between 30 and 39, 3 between 40 and 49, 4 between 50 and 59, 5 between 60 and 69, 6 between 70 and 79, and 7 over 80. For monthly income, 1 means less than $1000; 2 between $1000 and $2000; 3 between $2000 and $3000; 4 between $3000 and $4000; 5 between $4000 and $5000; 6 between $5000 and $6000; and 7 beyond $6000.

For education, 1 means primary education completed; 2 junior high school completed; 3 high school diploma; 4 bachelor's degree (including degree from community college); and 5 postgraduate. Gender (0 = male, 1 = female); marital status (0 = married, 1 = single, divorced, separated); and employment status (0 = yes, 1 = no) were suggested as dummy variables. Number of children and years lived in the community required actual numbers.

Individual community well-being indicators. The survey included questions of 34 individual community well-being indicators under 12 sectors (see Table 3.3) drawn from prior studies about community well-being indicators in Korea. A question required self-assessment of a given indicator on a scale of 1–10 (e.g. "How satisfied are you with the quality of educational service in your community?"). These self-assessed answers measured perceptions of 34 individual community well-being indicators.

Sense of community. The survey included two questions related to sense of community. One questioned sense of belonging and the other questioned intentionality of community involvement. Both questions were dummy variables: 0 meaning *no* and 1 meaning *yes*. The two variables were combined into one for the analysis. This method imposed a limitation on operationalization; we proceeded with the analysis in acknowledgement of this limitation.

Dependent variables. Two dependent variables were included for the multiple regression analysis: one was life satisfaction in the community, which is now referred to as subjective community well-being, and the other was satisfaction with local living conditions

- Satisfaction with local living conditions: How satisfied are you with living conditions in your local community?
- Subjective community well-being (life satisfaction in the community): Satisfaction with life in the community: How satisfied are you with your life in your local community?

Context of Two Areas: Sungmisan and Mapo

Located in Mapo municipality in Seoul, Korea, the Sungmisan community is a small community that surrounds a small hill known as Sungmisan, a community renowned for its vibrant grassroots civic networking. There are no clear-cut boundaries that demarcate the Sungmisan community from the rest of the municipality. Presumably between 1000 and 2000 people are populated in the community that stretches about 0.3–0.6 miles. The origin of Sungmisan community can be traced to an informal group that formed in 1994 whose purpose was to share the responsibility of babysitting among its members, which soon led to a babysitting co-op. As it became successful and the children grew older, other needs for alternative educational services emerged so the children could experience learning connected to the community in a holistic manner. In 2001, a group of community residents launched a community co-op (called *Mapo Doore Co-op*, currently *Woolim*; see http://woollim.org) that worked in bottom-up community development for the long term. Currently, the co-op engages in a variety of community entrepreneurial project beyond education: day care centers, afterschool programs, alternative schools, an automotive service center, a side-dishes store, a community radio station, a recycling center, a community café, a theater, a community building center, a disability resource center, and more. Sungmisan is one of the most often studied areas on grassroots community development. It was also named in Seoul as an exemplary model for such development. Mapo is one of 25 municipalities in Seoul and had a population of 393,576 in 2012.

Study Sample

Table 3.1 displays important descriptive information about Mapo and Sungmisan. In terms of the average age, Sungmisan residents (2.54) are younger than Mapo residents (3.58). The average years lived among Mapo respondents (16.4 years, 79 years the longest), was four times greater than the average years lived among Sungmisan residents (4.6 years, 20 years the longest). These differences may be indirect evidence of the history of the Sungmisan community, which began roughly twenty years back. Mapo had more married people than had Sungmisan and the ratio of male to female appeared to be nearly the same between the two. Sungmisan showed a higher education level than did Mapo, whereas Mapo showed a higher income level than did Sungmisan. Given general positive influences of education and income on personal well-being, Table 3.2 shows mean differences in income, education, and subjective SES between Sungmisan and Mapo. Only in education was there a significant difference: Sungmisan residents showed a higher level of education than Mapo residents ($p = 0.000$), while there were no significant differences in income and subjective SES. Another notable thing is that in age, years lived, education, and income, standard deviations of Sungmisan are nearly half those of Mapo, which discloses that Sungmian is a more homogenous community than is Mapo.

Findings

Mean Differences

Table 3.3 presents mean differences between Sungmisan and Mapo in 34 individual community well-being variables across 12 sectors, based on a t-test. For all except six indicators—garbage collection service, public transportation, Internet service, support for cultural art-related activities, public library, and attitude of public officials' performance—Sungmisan residents expressed higher satisfaction than did Mapo residents. In particular, mean differences in satisfaction with overall social welfare services, natural disaster services, public safety, police workforces, unemployment benefits/support, work conditions (individual), local government finance, budget operation, taxation, and overall local economic conditions exceeded 1. In community engagement and volunteerism, Sungmisan residents displayed higher ratings than did Mapo residents, which shows evidence of active community engagement in Sungmisan. Table 3.4 indicates that Sungmisan residents had a greater sense of belonging and intentionality of community involvement than had Mapo residents. These two variables are incorporated into one composite variable: sense of community.

The results in Table 3.5 show that Sungmisan residents were by and large more satisfied with local living conditions than were Mapo residents. Yet,

Table 3.1 Descriptive data of Mapo and Sungmisan: age, years lived, marital status, education, gender, and income

	Mapo					Sungmisan				
	N	Min.	Max.	Mean	Std. deviation	N	Min.	Max.	Mean	Std. deviation
Age	186	2	7	3.58	1.859	128	1	4	2.54	0.995
Years lived	182	1	79	16.41	15.949	120	1	20	4.6	3.289
Marital status	178	0	1	0.31	0.466	127	0	1	0.4	0.492
Education	182	1	5	3.25	1.056	128	1	5	4.07	0.689
Gender	195	0	1	0.47	0.500	128	0	1	0.49	0.502
Income	152	1	7	3.81	1.876	120	1	3.71	6.58	0.965

#: $p = 0.1$, * $p = 0.05$, ** $p < 0.01$, *** $p = 0.000$

Table 3.2 Mean differences in income, education, and subjective SES

	Education		Income		Subjective SES	
District	Mapo	Sungmisan	Mapo	Sungmisan	Mapo	Sungmisan
Mean	3.25	4.07***	6.68	6.58	4.39	4.65
N	182	128	152	120	170	120

#: $p = 0.1$, * $p = 0.05$, ** $p < 0.01$, *** $p = 0.0001$

Table 3.3 Mean differences in community well-being indicators between Mapo and Sungmisan

	Satisfaction	Mapo	Sungmisan	Mean difference	Sig.
Health	Health condition (individual)	6.36	**6.7#**	−0.345	0.084
	Medical service	6.09	**6.47#**	−0.378	0.06
Environment	Garbage collection service	6.28	6.18	0.101	0.645
	Air quality	5.47	**6.71*** **	−1.243	0.000
	Green spaces	5.92	**6.55*** **	−0.627	0.008
Transportation and internet	Public transportation	6.54	6.73	−0.188	0.416
	Internet service	6.47	6.44	0.031	0.872
	Road conditions	5.9	**6.7*** **	−0.801	0.000
Culture	Cultural art-related activities (individual)	6.02	**6.83*** **	−0.808	0.000
	Cultural art-related activities (community)	5.87	**6.45***	−0.577	0.012
	Support for cultural-art activities	5.61	5.86	−0.256	0.254
Education	Public library	5.75	5.99	−0.238	0.275
	Lifelong learning service	5.6	**6.46*** **	−0.857	0.000
	Education environment	5.75	**6.68*** **	−0.929	0.000
Social welfare provided by local government	Services for seniors	6.07	**6.47#**	−0.401	0.062
	Services for the disabled	5.8	**6.44#**	−0.645	0.097
	Childcare services	5.48	6.47***	−0.994	0.000
	Overall social welfare services	5.82	6.38**	−0.557	0.008
Local public services	Fairness of public officials' performances	5.8	6.48**	−0.676	0.002
	Attitude of public officials' performance	6.14	6.41	−0.266	0.22
	Overall satisfaction for public services	5.91	**7.04*** **	−1.133	0.000

(continued)

Table 3.3 (continued)

	Satisfaction	Mapo	Sungmisan	Mean difference	Sig.
Public safety	Natural disaster preparedness	5.7	**6.9*****	−1.198	0.000
	Public safety	5.61	**6.65*****	−1.041	0.000
	Police workforce	5.35	**6.85*****	−1.504	0.000
Community involvement	Community engagement	5.87	**6.55*****	−0.676	0.001
	Volunteerism	5.76	**6.32****	−0.552	0.007
Employment	Vocational training	5.27	**6.21*****	−0.938	0.000
	Unemployment benefits/ support	5.04	**6.62*****	−1.58	0.000
	Work condition (individual)	5.29	**6.56*****	−1.266	0.000
Local economy I	Local government finance	5.08	**6.55*****	−1.47	0.000
	Budget operations	5.01	**6.58*****	−1.572	0.000
	Taxation	5.00	**6.55*****	−1.555	0.000
Local economy II	Overall local economic conditions	5.21	**6.26*****	−1.055	0.000
	Local living cost	5.61	**6.27*****	−0.655	0.001

Table 3.4 Sense of belonging and intentionality of community involvement

	Sense of belonging		Intentionality of community involvement	
District	Mapo	Sungmisan	Mapo	Sungmisan
Mean	0.58	0.76**	0.43	0.78***
N	162	127	157	125

[#]: $p = 0.1$, * $p = 0.05$, ** $p = 0.01$, *** $p = 0.0001$

Table 3.5 Satisfaction for local living conditions and subjective community well-being (life satisfaction in the community)

	Mapo	Sungmisan	Mean difference	Sig.
Overall satisfaction with local living conditions	5.69	6.47***	−0.776	0.000
Subjective community well-being (life satisfaction in the community)	**6.53[#]**	6.17	0.357	0.072

[#]: $p = 0.1$, * $p = 0.05$, ** $p = 0.01$, *** $p = 0.0001$

Mapo residents expressed higher life subjective community well-being than did Sungmisan residents.

Table 3.6 presents bivariate correlations between sense of community, satisfaction with local living conditions, and subjective community well-being. Satisfaction with local living conditions is fairly correlated with sense of community in both Mapo and Sungmisan. In Mapo, sense of community showed a significant correlation only in satisfaction with local living conditions, but in Sungmisan, sense of community was significantly correlated with both satisfaction with local living conditions and subjective community well-being.

Table 3.6 Bivariate correlations between sense of community, satisfaction with local living conditions, and subjective community well-being

	Mapo			Sungmisan		
	(1)	(2)	(3)	(1)	(2)	(3)
1. Sense of community	1			1		
2. Satisfaction with local living conditions	0.200*	1		0.279**	1	
3. Subjective community well-being	0.98	0.468**	1	0.173#	0.413**	1

#: $p = 0.1$, * $p = 0.05$, ** $p = 0.01$, *** $p = 0.0001$, two-tailed

The Role of Sense of Community

Multiple regression analysis was used to examine the influence of sense of community on the two dependent variables: satisfaction with local living conditions and subjective community well-being (life satisfaction in the community). Instead of all 34 variables, twelve variables representing each sector were used in the model, as well as demographic variables and a composite variable regarding sense of community.

Satisfaction with local living conditions. In Mapo, medical services, unemployment benefits/support, years lived in the community, and age appeared to have significant influences on overall satisfaction with local living conditions. Only age had a negative coefficient, which suggests younger people are more likely to have greater overall satisfaction than older ones with local living conditions (see Table 3.7).

In Sungmisan, cultural and arts-related activities (on the community level), overall social welfare services, public safety, community involvement, and sense of community had significant influences on overall satisfaction with local living conditions. Both the variables of community involvement and sense of community showed strong to moderate positive influences on satisfaction with local living conditions. Interestingly, though, overall social welfare services had a negative influence on satisfaction with local living conditions. Technically, this result means that those who are less satisfied with overall social welfare services provided by the local government tend to display higher subjective community well-being. This, however, should be interpreted with caution, and is revisited in the discussion section.

Subjective community well-being (life satisfaction in the community). In Mapo, medical services, income, and gender had positive influences on subjective community well-being. That is, residents who expressed higher satisfaction with medical services, earned higher income, and were female, were more likely to show a higher level of subjective community well-being.

In Sungmisan, public safety and age had a significant influence on subjective community well-being. The standardized coefficient for public safety was 0.326, while the one for age was −0.231, which implies that residents who are younger and express higher satisfaction with public safety are more likely than

Table 3.7 Satisfaction of local living conditions

	Mapo				Sungmisan			
	Unstandardized coefficients		Std. coefficients	Sig.	Unstandardized coefficients		Std. coefficients	Sig.
	B	Std. error	Beta		B	Std. error	Beta	
(Constant)	−0.109	0.969		0.911	−0.259	1.303		0.843
Medical service	0.197	0.100	0.211#	0.051	0.113	0.120	0.104	0.346
Air quality	0.123	0.092	0.122	0.185	0.048	0.106	0.049	0.653
Public transportation	0.056	0.072	0.072	0.433	−0.016	0.133	−0.014	0.903
Cultural-art activities (community)	−0.056	0.087	−0.069	0.523	0.259	0.111	0.252*	0.022
Education environment	0.114	0.085	0.138	0.183	0.168	0.143	0.141	0.243
Overall social welfare services	−0.019	0.095	−0.022	0.842	−0.440	0.145	−0.357**	0.003
Attitude of public officials' performance	0.094	0.093	0.111	0.316	−0.004	0.131	−0.003	0.977
Public safety	0.132	0.080	0.151	0.101	0.347	0.140	0.301*	0.015
Community involvement	−0.006	0.104	−0.006	0.958	0.351	0.122	0.333**	0.005
Unemployment benefits/support	0.170	0.094	0.176#	0.074	−0.003	0.142	−0.003	0.981
Taxation	0.052	0.099	0.055	0.603	−0.144	0.148	−0.127	0.336
Overall local economic conditions	0.129	0.097	0.133	0.186	0.146	0.170	0.124	0.393
Years lived in the community	0.799	0.340	0.218**	0.021	0.212	0.386	0.048	0.585
Sense of community	0.074	0.344	0.017	0.829	0.798	0.412	0.177#	0.057
Age	−0.213	0.118	−0.219#	0.073	0.021	0.161	0.013	0.898
Education	−0.026	0.146	−0.014	0.862	0.003	0.184	0.002	0.986
Income	0.099	0.068	0.101	0.148	0.162	0.146	0.106	0.271
Gender	0.089	0.250	0.024	0.724	−0.246	0.265	−0.083	0.357
Marital status	−0.289	0.384	−0.076	0.454	0.077	0.303	0.025	0.801
Adjusted R²	0.561				0.447			

#: $p = 0.1$, *: $p = 0.05$, **: $p = 0.01$, ***: $p = 0.0001$

older people to express greater subjective community well-being. However, sense of community appeared to have a significant influence on subjective community well-being neither in Mapo nor in Sungmisan. Interestingly, satisfaction with overall social welfare services had a strong negative influence on subjective community well-being again. We further discuss this issue in the section that follows (Table 3.8).

Discussion

In this study, we explored how sense of community influences subjective community well-being by comparing two communities—Sungmisan and Mapo—that exhibited contrasting traits but were assumed to have experienced the same objective community well-being in terms of local public services. Sungmisan is a small community geographically nested in Mapo, which implies that technically Sungmisan and Mapo experience the same local public services. Furthermore, Sungmisan fits the conventional notion of a small community with no official boundaries or eligibility for membership better than does Mapo. Its demarcation and communal narrative have been historically developed and shared among community residents, and the descriptive data found more homogeneity in Sungmisan than in Mapo.

These features tied with the conventional notion of community were hardly observed in Mapo—an area at the census track level—that includes a number of heterogeneous neighborhoods and a population of almost 400,000 people, as well as a much larger territory and official boundaries. In the comparisons of individual community well-being indicators, Sungmisan residents showed higher satisfaction in 28 items out of 34. Sungmisan residents also expressed a greater sense of belonging and satisfaction with local living conditions than did Mapo residents. However, Mapo residents expressed experiencing greater subjective community well-being than Sungmisan residents did, which was the opposite of the expectations we had before conducting the survey. We had assumed that a smaller community with a high level of sense of community would show a greater level of subjective community well-being.

Although the results contradicted our initial expectations, they still provided important insights in understanding community well-being and the role of sense of community. In Mapo, which had expressed a lesser sense of community than did Sungmisan, subjective community well-being was influenced largely by medical services and income, a trend closer to conventional social welfare indicators. This tendency is consistent with the result of Mapo's satisfaction with local living conditions: those who are more satisfied with medical services and unemployment benefits/support tend to be more satisfied with local living conditions. Importantly, medical services and unemployment benefits/support typically fall into conventional social welfare domains, for they are controlled more by a central government than by local governments.

Table 3.8 Subjective community well-being between Mapo and Sungmisan

	Mapo				Sungmisan			
	Unstandardized coefficients		Std. coefficients	Sig.	Unstandardized coefficients		Std. coefficients	Sig.
	B	Std. error	Beta		B	Std. error	Beta	
(Constant)	3.431	1.229		0.006	2.848	1.560		0.072
Medical service	0.281	0.126	0.319*	0.029	−0.025	0.143	−0.022	0.864
Air quality	0.085	0.117	0.091	0.465	0.104	0.127	0.105	0.413
Public transportation	−0.082	0.092	−0.110	0.379	−0.098	0.159	−0.084	0.540
Cultural-art activities (community)	0.044	0.111	0.058	0.690	0.121	0.133	0.115	0.366
Education environment	0.006	0.110	0.008	0.953	0.121	0.171	0.100	0.479
Overall social welfare services	−0.038	0.122	−0.046	0.759	−0.303	0.174	−0.242#	0.086
Attitude of public officials' performance	−0.010	0.118	−0.012	0.934	0.051	0.157	0.043	0.744
Public safety	0.021	0.107	0.025	0.845	0.382	0.167	0.326*	0.025
Community involvement	−0.044	0.132	−0.048	0.737	0.244	0.146	0.228	0.100
Unemployment benefits/support	0.111	0.123	0.121	0.370	−0.039	0.171	−0.033	0.818
Taxation	0.151	0.126	0.170	0.236	−0.250	0.177	−0.217	0.164
Overall local economic conditions	−0.074	0.123	−0.081	0.547	0.153	0.204	0.127	0.456
Years lived in the community	0.441	0.434	0.128	0.312	0.532	0.463	0.119	0.254
Sense of community	−0.291	0.437	−0.071	0.507	0.284	0.494	0.062	0.567
Age	0.026	0.150	0.028	0.865	−0.382	0.193	−0.231#	0.052
Education	−0.266	0.186	−0.160	0.156	0.222	0.220	0.107	0.315
Income	0.235	0.086**	0.257**	0.008	0.079	0.175	0.051	0.654
Gender	0.703	0.318*	0.203*	0.029	−0.503	0.318	−0.166	0.118
Marital status	0.253	0.490	0.070	0.607	−0.367	0.363	−0.118	0.315
Adjusted R square		0.200				0.232		

#: $p = 0.1$, * $p = 0.05$, ** $p = 0.01$, *** $p = 0.0001$

Because we were ultimately interested in explaining the role of sense of community in subjective community well-being, we closely observed Sungmisan's data for unique trends that would differentiate Sungmisan from Mapo. As seen in the previous section, Sungmisan provided interesting results. First, sense of community had a positive influence on satisfaction with local living conditions, but not on subjective community well-being (life satisfaction in the community). Among several possible reasons, we speculate that a sense of community had a stronger correlation with local living conditions than with subjective community well-being (see Table 3.6), and this influence may have been reflected in the regression analyses. This speculation currently is without evidence; thus, further investigation is needed to determine the sophisticated relationships across those variables.

Second, besides one individual variable, the variables that appeared to be significant for either or both dependent variable(s) in Sungmisan were community environment-related variables: public safety, community cultural art-related activities, and community involvement, besides sense of community, which illustrates a unique characteristic of Sungmisan. The area is highly community-oriented, and is also in striking contrast with Mapo where the significant variables are categorized as conventional social welfare services (such as medical services and unemployment benefits/support) controlled more by a central government than by local governments, as well as individual variables (income, age, and gender).

For instance, strong associations of public safety with both dependent variables (satisfaction with local living conditions and subjective community well-being) in Sungmisan can be evidence of a close-knit community. One can guess that Sungmisan is a small community, where everyone knows each other. This environment makes visitors or strangers easily noticeable for their close network functions as an informal and effective public safety net for residents, especially for children. Community cultural art-related activities and community involvement could also be strong indicators of a community-oriented nature in Sungmisan.

Significantly, the negative influences of overall social welfare services on both dependent variables in Sungmisan—subjective community well-being and satisfaction with local living conditions—are in question. This result suggests that the less satisfied residents are with overall social welfare services (provided by local governments), the more satisfied they are with their life in the community and with their local living conditions. We, however, do not accept this result to be a general rule. One possible interpretation is that because Sungmisan residents are already satisfied with life in the community for some reason (having already established good assets or networks themselves), they may not feel a need for social welfare services (provided by local government). That is, they turn away from these "governmental institutions" and rely on community/grassroots assets, which may lead them to a negative bias against welfare. We can conclude that even this negative influence eventually supports the community-oriented nature of Sungmisan regarding local living conditions and subjective well-being. Nonetheless, this interpretation is not supported by solid evidence, and we suggest further examination to discover the underlying causes for this seemingly unusual relationship.

Although Mapo revealed a higher level of subjective community well-being than did Sungmisan, Sungmisan showed higher satisfaction in 28 items out of 34 individual community well-being indicators. In particular, in Sungmisan, sense of community and other community-level variables play a role in subjective community well-being, as well as satisfaction with local living conditions.

While sense of community has rarely seen the limelight in community well-being research, this paper supports the premise that subjective community well-being is not solely determined by an external state (objective community well-being), but can be shaped by sense of community. As previous researchers have noted, sense of community has complicated relationships with various variables: age, income, years of lived in the community, marital status, number of children, and the nature of the community (size, population density, structure of predominant buildings, ethnicity, and more). Further research needs to be done to elucidate the relationships of sense of community not only with subjective community well-being, but also with the elements that influence it, including those listed previously.

This study discloses several limitations. Specifically, sense of community was not so formally defined and incorporated into the survey used in this study. A more thorough conceptualization should be developed drawing upon previous literature. Moreover, what seemed to be more problematic was that sense of community was given as a dummy variable ($0 = no$, $1 = yes$). A larger and continuous scale should be adopted for the next survey, and these scales would contribute to a more complete explanation of the role of sense of community in community well-being.

Finally, and importantly, we suggest that qualitative approaches be considered, which offer a different perspective for understanding the complex issues involved. For example, regarding the negative association between overall social welfare service and subjective community well-being in Sungmisan, possible questions for qualitative research are as follows: "What do you mean by local living in Sungmisan?" "To what extent is community important in their lives of residents in the community?" "What do social welfare services provided by a local government mean to you?" and "What do you think about the role of local government in regard to community well-being?" These questions can also be applied to Mapo residents and the answers would make a good comparison with those for Sungmisan. Such questions will lead to a fuller explanation of the dynamics surrounding sense of community and community well-being.

Conclusion

Sungmisan is a small grassroots community within Mapo known for having a strong civic network among its residents. Sungmisan and Mapo are assumed to possess similar objective community well-being in terms of local public services (i.e., education, mass transportation, trash services, etc.). The research described in this paper reveals a greater sense of community among Sungmisan residents compared to that among Mapo residents.

Contrary to our initial assumption, subjective community well-being was observed to be greater in Mapo than it was in Sungmisan, and not established as a significant variable for subjective community well-being for Sungmisan (yet significant for satisfaction with local living conditions). Nonetheless, our findings showed that Sungmisan demonstrated highly community-oriented characteristics, as opposed to Mapo. In Sungmisan, community-related variables including community cultural-art activities and community involvement were found to be significant in determining subjective community well-being and satisfaction with local living conditions. By contrast, in the case of Mapo, it turned out that medical services and income—closer to conventional social welfare indicators and under a central government's jurisdiction—were positively associated with subjective community well-being and satisfaction with local living conditions.

These findings partially repeat the results of previous research: sense of community has a positive influence on satisfaction with local living conditions (not confirmed for subjective community well-being, though). Still, they reveal significant issues for future research, especially the need to take into account community-level characteristics, the notion of sense of community, and relationships with community well-being and individual community well-being indicators. Such research will contribute to a more advanced theorization of community well-being.

Acknowledgments This chapter was presentesd at the 3rd International Forum on Community Well-being on June 23rd, 2015 at the Hoam Faculty House, Seoul, South Korea and was supported by the National Research Foundation of Korea Grant funded by the Korean Government (NRF-2013S1A3A2054622).

References

Benson, M., & Jackson, E. (2013). Place-making and place maintenance: Performativity, place and belonging among the middle classes. *Sociology, 47*(4), 793–809.

Cornelio, G. S., & Ardévol, E. (2011). Practices of place-making through locative media artworks. *Communications, 36*(3), 313–333.

Cox, D., Frere, M., West, S., & Wiseman, J. (2010). Developing and using local community well-being indicators: Learning from the experience of Community Indicators Victoria. *Australian Journal of Social Issues, 45*(1), 71–88. (Australian Council of Social Service).

Cummins, R. A., Eckersley, R., Pallant, J., van Jackie, V., & Misajon, R. (2003). Developing a national index of subjective well-being: The Australian unity well-being index. *Social Indicators Research, 64*(2), 160–190.

Cuthill, M. (2002). Coolangatta: A portrait of community well-being. *Urban Policy & Research, 20*(2), 187–203.

Davidson, W. B., & Cotter, P. R. (1986). Measurement of sense of community within the sphere of city. *Journal of Applied Social Psychology, 16*(7), 608–619.

de Certeau, M. (1984). *The practice of everyday life*. Berkeley, Los Angeles: University of California Press.

Easterlin, R. (1995). Will raising the incomes of all increase the happiness of all? *Journal of Economic Behavior & Organization, 27*, 35–47.

Farrell, S. J., Aubry, T., & Coulombe, D. (2004). Neighborhoods and neighbors: Do they contribute to personal well-being? *Journal of Community Psychology, 32*(1), 9–25.

Fried, M. (1984). The structure and significance of community satisfaction. *Population and Environment, 7*(2), 61–86.

Gusfield, J. R. (1975). *The community: A critical response*. New York: Harper Colophon Books.

Hombrados-Mendieta, M. I., Gomez-Jacinto, L., Dominguez-Fuentes, J. M., & Garcia-Leiva, P. (2013). Sense of community and satisfaction with life among immigrants and the native population. *Journal of Community Psychology, 41*(5), 601–614.

Hooghe, M., & Vanhoutte, B. (2011). Subjective well-being and social capital in Belgian communities: The impact of community characteristics on subjective well-being indicators in Belgium. *Social Indicators Research, 100*(1), 17–36.

Jorgensen, B. S., & Stedman, R. C. (2001). Sense of place as an attitude: Lakeshore owners attitudes toward their properties. *Journal of Environmental Psychology, 21*(3), 233–248.

Kim, Y., & Lee, S. J. (2013). The development and application of a community well-being index in Korean metropolitan cities. *Social Indicators Research*, 1–26.

Leander, K. M., & McKim, K. K. (2003). Tracing the everyday 'sitings' of adolescents on the internet: A strategic adaptation of ethnography across online and offline spaces. *Education, Communication & Information, 3*(2), 211.

Mak, W. S., Cheung, R. M., & Law, L. C. (2009). Sense of community in Hong Kong: Relations with community-level characteristics and residents' well-being. *American Journal of Community Psychology, 44*(1–2), 80–92.

McMillian, D., & Chavis, D. (1986). Sense of community: A definition and theory. *Journal of Community Psychology, 14*, 6–23.

Pierce, J., Martin, D. G., & Murphy, J. T. (2011). Relational place-making: The networked politics of place. *Transactions of the Institute of British Geographers, 36*(1), 54–70.

Pink, S. (2008). Mobilising visual ethnography: Making routes, making place and making images. *Forum: Qualitative Social Research, 9*(3), 1–17.

Prezza, M., Amici, M., Roberti, T., & Tedeschi, G. (2001). Sense of community referred to the whole town: Its relations with neighboring, loneliness, life satisfaction, and area of residence. *Journal of Community Psychology, 29*(1), 29–52.

Prezza, M., & Costantini, S. (1998). Sense of community and life satisfaction: Investigation in three different territorial contexts. *Journal of Community & Applied Social Psychology, 8*(3), 181–194.

Sarason, S. B. (1974). *The psychological sense of community: Prospects for community psychology*. San Francisco, CA: Jossey Bass.

Shamai, S., & Ilatov, Z. (2005). Measuring sense of place: Methodological aspects. *Tijdschrift voor Economische en Sociale Geografie (Journal of Economic & Social Geography), 96*(5), 467–476.

Sirgy, M., Widgery, R., Lee, D.-J., & Yu, G. (2010). Developing a measure of community well-being based on perceptions of impact in various life domains. *Social Indicators Research, 96*(2), 295–311.

Swain, D., & Hollar, D. (2003). Measuring progress: Community indicators and the quality of life. *International Journal of Public Administration, 26*(7), 789–796.

Chapter 4
The Development and Production of Local, National and International State of Children's Well-Being Report Cards

Geoffrey Woolcock

Abstract The idea of local communities identifying and reporting on key indicators for children and young people is attracting significant attention as a model for many communities across the Asia-Pacific region. A number of these communities have leveraged their work through an association with the UNICEF Child-Friendly Cities model and/or government-funded place-based initiatives, all using various data and well-being reports as a foundational tool for their planning and monitoring. Other communities have looked to the enormous investment in standardized indices or national well-being scorecards to further the interest in how their own children and young people are faring. There is also a growing understanding internationally that 'place-based' and local responses are essential in responding to disadvantage and community well-being.

Keywords Indicators · Children's well-being · Scorecards

This chapter establishes a sound, rigorous basis for demonstrating how well-being outcomes for children and young people are measured and impact at the local community scale through an overview of a diverse range of social contexts in which such measures are being applied.

Introduction

The highly regarded UNICEF Child-Friendly Cities worldwide initiative identifies 9 building blocks for creating a child-friendly community (http://childfriendlycities.org/building-a-cfc/building-blocks/). While all the

G. Woolcock (✉)
Wesley Mission Brisbane, Brisbane, Australia
e-mail: g.woolcock@wmb.org.au

© Springer International Publishing Switzerland 2016
Y. Kee et al. (eds.), *Social Factors and Community Well-Being*,
SpringerBriefs in Well-Being and Quality of Life Research,
DOI 10.1007/978-3-319-29942-6_4

building blocks are regarded as equally important, progress in any one area is destined to be limited without establishing baseline measures of how children and young people are faring in any community.

The idea of local communities identifying and reporting on key indicators for children and young people is attracting significant attention as a model for many communities across the Asia-Pacific. Many communities are creating local 'governance' structures for ensuring coordination of effort for children and young people's well-being.

A number of these communities have leveraged their work through an association with the UNICEF Child-Friendly Cities model and/or government-funded place-based initiatives, all using various data and well-being reports as a foundational tool for their planning and monitoring. Other communities have looked to the enormous investment in standardized indices (e.g. Australian Early Development Index www.aedi.org.au) or national well-being scorecards (e.g. via the Australian Research Alliance for Children and Youth ARACY) to further the interest in how their own children and young people are faring. Many 'investors' such as government and philanthropic foundations are also interested in planning tools that assist them in prioritising how to invest strategically in long-term outcomes for children and young people. There is also a growing understanding internationally that 'place-based' and local responses are essential in responding to disadvantage and community well-being. Such investors are also committed to finding ways that ensure their investment builds local capacity, local leadership and leverages shared investment, utilizing scorecards or benchmarks of children's well-being.

This chapter establishes a sound, rigorous basis for demonstrating how well-being outcomes for children and young people are measured and impact at the local community scale through an overview of a diverse range of social contexts in which such measures are being applied.

In recent years, there has been an increase in the number of indicators and reporting frameworks that are used to report on the health and welfare of children and young people, in Australia and internationally, thereby creating a rich reporting environment. This surge of interest reflects not only a widespread interest in the well-being of children but also a growing recognition of the importance of reporting on a wide range of indicators to inform policy development (Ben-Arieh 2008; Brown and Moore 2009; Klocke et al. 2014). Another reflection of the growing children's well-being indicator field is the emergence of the International Society of Child Indicators (ISCI), a professional society dedicated to the exchange of information among people working in this field.

Infants, children and young people (aged 0–24) made up about a third of most of the OECD member nation populations. They form a distinct group within the population, with particular health and social needs that require access to a range of services. What happens in the early years of a child's life is critical, and this period provides the foundation for future health, development and well-being of the individual. It also shapes the future health and productivity of the whole population. Tackling health and well-being problems when they occur in childhood and adolescence is socially and economically more effective than dealing with enduring problems in adulthood. Many attitudes, behaviours and even illnesses that largely determine adult health and well-being, have their origins in childhood, adolescence and early adulthood. Adolescence and young adulthood are critical periods for reinforcing positive health and social behaviours, as behaviours at this age are strong predictors of behaviours in later life (Muir et al. 2009).

Indicators of children's well-being are increasingly used by child advocacy groups, policymakers, researchers, the media, and service providers for several purposes including to describe the condition of children, to monitor or track child outcomes, or to set goals. Although there are notable gaps and inadequacies in existing child and family well-being indicators, there also are literally dozens of data series and indicators from which to form opinions and draw conclusions (Ben-Arieh and Goerge 2006). The rapidly growing interest in children's well-being indicators stems, in part, from a movement toward accountability-based public policy, which demands more accurate measures of the conditions children face and the outcomes of various programs designed to address those conditions. At the same time, the rapid changes in family life also have prompted an increased demand from child development professionals, social scientists, and the public for a better picture of children's well-being.

In addition to the growing policy demands for accountability, the birth and development of the child indicators movement can be attributed to the emergence of new normative and conceptual theories as well as methodological advancements. Broadly speaking, Ben-Arieh (2008) identifies three major normative or theoretical changes have contributed to the creation and evolution of the child indicators field: (1) the normative concept of children rights; (2) the new sociology of childhood as a stage in and of itself; and (3) ecological theories of child development. Similarly, three methodological issues gave rise to the child indicators movement: (1) the emerging importance of the subjective perspective; (2) the child as the unit of observation; and (3) the expanded use of administrative data and the growing variety of data sources. Finally, the call for more policy-oriented research also played a role in this evolution.

National Children's Well-Being Indicators

Ideally, a national system of indicators should provide an accurate picture of the well-being of children and young people, and be an effective tool for informing policy development and evaluation. To achieve this, it needs to have a comprehensive coverage with respect to the indicators and population groups it includes (Moore 1997). Most importantly, it should feature:

- A broad range of indicators that capture all the factors that are important to the well-being and development of children and young people
- data for all relevant age, social, geographic and ethnic groups, including children/young people with disability

- reporting that is regular and frequent enough to be relevant to governments on short policy cycles
- results that are readily available to policy makers, researchers, journalists and the general public.

Wherever possible, different reporting frameworks that include similar indicators should use and define these consistently to facilitate direct comparisons of the results they report. Consistent use of indicators is also critical to enable evaluation of policy measures and tracking of change over time.

In addition to national frameworks, international frameworks also compare the performance of different countries. By highlighting the relative strengths and weaknesses of comparable countries, these frameworks are particularly valuable as guides to areas that need attention from policy makers. To be included, each country needs to make data available that conform to the indicators in the international framework. The leading international comparison of children's well-being in developed countries *Child well-being in rich countries: A comparative overview* is published as Innocenti Report cards by the UNICEF Research Office. This framework used as its starting point the UN Convention on the Rights of the Child. At present, Australia is excluded from the ranking tables of this report because it has data for fewer than 75 % of the total number of indicators used (UNICEF 2013).

Of course, it ought to be acknowledged that considerable interest continues to be sustained in the comparison of national children's well-being measures. Perhaps the most relevant overview is Lau and Bradshaw's (2010) study extending previous efforts to compare the well-being of children using multi-dimensional indicators derived from sample survey and administrative series to thirteen countries in the Pacific Rim. The framework for the analysis of child well-being organised 46 indicators into 21 components and then organised the components into six domains: material situation, health, education, subjective well-being, living environment, as well as risk and safety. Overall, Japan, Singapore and Taiwan have the highest child well-being and Thailand, Indonesia and the Philippines the lowest. However, substantial variations exist between the domains with Japan and Korea performing best on the material well-being of children and also do well on health and education but having the lowest subjective well-being among their children by some margin. Furthermore, there is a relationship between child well-being and GDP per capita but children in China have higher well-being than you would expect given their GDP and children in Australia have lower well-being.

In Australia, the publication of national children's well-being indicators has been extensive. The Key National Indicators of Child Health, Development and Well-being (Key Child National Indicators or KC) provide a comprehensive overview of the health, development and well-being of Australia's children. The indicators are underpinned by the National Child Health Information Framework, a conceptual framework for the organisation of national child health information. The framework was developed at a workshop convened by the Australian Institute of Health and Welfare (AIHW) in 1998, and subsequently endorsed by the Australian Health Ministers' Advisory Council (AHMAC). The indicators are reported in *A picture of Australia's children*, of which there have been 5 editions (1996, 2002, 2005, 2009 and 2012). The framework was revised for the 2005 edition, expanded for the 2009 edition and retained unaltered for the 2012 edition. The publications (also available electronically) serve as compendiums and provide interpretive commentary as well as contextual and supplementary data. The latest edition (2012) has an accompanying web product, with one web page devoted to each topic area.

There are 56 indicators across 7 topic areas (health, child development, learning, risk factors, family and community, safety and system performance). This framework aims to cover the age range of 0–14 years and to include disaggregation for sex, age (0–4, 5–9 and 10–14 years), Indigenous status, remoteness and socioeconomic groups. When possible, it also includes international comparisons.

Following the endorsement of the *Headline Indicators for Children's Health, Development and Well-being in 2006* (see below) the Key Child National Indicators also incorporated a number of relevant Headline Indicators (HI) in 2009. As a result, the Headline Indicators currently constitutes a subset of the Key Child National Indicators. A number of more recently developed frameworks also discussed in this report have drawn on indicators from the Key Child National Indicators (e.g. the Early Childhood Development Outcome Measures Framework and the National Framework for Protecting Australia's Children). The Headline Indicators have also been well informed by the long-standing Longitudinal Study of Australian Children (LSAC) for which indices were developed to fill the need for indicators suitable for use by diverse data users in order to guide government policy and interventions which support young children's optimal development (Sanson et al. 2010).

Small Area Data as a Catalyst for Local Children's Well-Being Reports

Coulton et al. (2009) highlight why those interested in child well-being should direct attention to small area indicators. Small areas (for example, villages, neighbourhoods and communities) are the immediate context in which families and children live. Attention to small areas allows for a more nuanced and contextual understanding of deprivation, social exclusion, and disparities than is possible in analyses at the state or national level. At a state or national level, differences may be muted in the portrayal child indicators as rates on measures of well-being. Overall rates of infant mortality in Australia, for example, may mask important sub-population differences in indigenous communities. Comparisons across small areas can reveal disparities in child well-being as well as point to strategies to reduce place-based inequalities.

Importantly, indices of child well-being at the small area level have implications for linking research, practice and policy. At the small area level, there is potential for the application of data to solutions as the data are made available to communities as well as to researchers. Bringing indicators to the small area level, such as community or neighbourhood, has the potential to engage citizens and non-related adults in promoting the well-being of children where they can take a personal interest and become engaged. National or State level data may be too far removed from the experience of daily living to engage citizens. Small area indicators, then, may be seen as enhancing civic engagement around concerns for children's well-being.

Data Functionality

Other scholars have pointed to the need for practically useful data sets to assist children's services seeking to improve children's well-being. Axford et al. (2013) in particular forcefully argue in the context of the United Kingdom that directors and service commissioners working in children's services need certain *types* of child well-being data, packaged in a particular way, and accompanied by specified methods to enable the analysis of that data as a basis for decision-making. They contend that this will help them to perform important functions that they struggle with presently—certainly outside of health services—because the data is not fit for purpose or packaged unhelpfully, or because the tools for exploiting it are unavailable. These functions include:

- prioritising which outcomes to address;
- deciding the balance between universal and targeted provision;
- determining the size of the target group and estimating demand;
- designing services (which includes selecting programmes to invest in);
- estimating realistic achievable change;
- reallocating resources towards prevention and early intervention; and
- monitoring trends.

Other scholars have identified key contemporary influences on measuring children's well-being that are highly relevant for the development and production of local children's well-being reports. Fattore et al. (2009) focus on children's views of what constitutes well-being, what meaning children and young people ascribe to the concept and whether distinct dimensions or characteristics of well-being can be identified. The major findings from the research include the overarching importance of relationships with others and, more specifically, the importance of agency and control in the various domains identified as relevant to their well-being, the importance of safety and security and the way these factors contribute to sense of self. More minor but significant domains identified were: dealing with adversity, material and economic resources, physical environments, physical health and social and moral responsibility. Others such as Abello et al. (2012) address more technical issues in their study of social exclusion indicators, acknowledging that despite great concern about child well-being, and an increasing recognition of the need to monitor how well children are doing, small area measures of child disadvantage are a very recent development in understanding child well-being both within Australia and internationally.

Data as a Means of Direct Community Engagement

Central to all the collaborative approaches attempting to coordinate place-based children's well-being strategies is the powerful role data plays in the process. A particularly engaging way of using data is to produce regular 'Children's Well-being Reports' both to catalyse action and to monitor progress.

A regular, locally-based children and youth well-being report has a number of benefits:

- Local children's service providers and funders use the data to identify deficits and opportunities that inform their planning and resource allocation decisions.
- It brings a wide range of organisations together to plan and prioritise action.
- As the community itself chooses what indicators are its priority, the public report and associated planning processes reinforces local shared responsibility for solving local issues.
- It makes the work of the collaboration publically accountable.
- It assists funders to prioritise resource allocation.

A number of local state of children's well-being reports have been initiated in the past decade, some as part of ongoing whole of community indicator reports (e.g. Vital Signs, Vancouver) and others across counties or sub-national regions (e.g. Hur and Testerman 2012). However, the context that is most familiar for this author is that of several Australian local communities that have participated in the UNICEF building child-friendly cities process and the clear standout is the city of Bendigo in the state of Victoria, some 90 min travelling time north of Melbourne, with a population of some 100,000.

Case Study: Bendigo, Australia

In 2007, the city of Bendigo in central Victoria was the first city in Australia to be granted Child Friendly City status by UNICEF (UNICEF 2011). Two years later, St Luke's Anglicare established a Bendigo Child Friendly City Leadership Group to coordinate effort across the Local Government, the community sector, State Government departments, business and other critical stakeholders working with children and young people. One of the Leadership Group's most significant achievements to date has been establishing a set of indicators to galvanise action, support strategic planning and monitor progress (UNICEF 2011). This case study outlines the process undertaken to produce the indicator set, released as *The State of Bendigo's Children Report* (Pope and Nolan 2011), as a lesson for others who may wish to replicate it.

A Strong Authorising Environment and Networks that Bring in Capacity

The Bendigo Child Friendly City Leadership Group provides a forum for organisations involved in improving the well-being of children and young people to discuss ideas for implementing the nine UNICEF principles for a Child Friendly City (UNICEF 2011). It recognises that impacting on the well-being of children and young people is complex and will require the combined efforts of government, the non-government sector, business and the community itself. One of the Leadership Group's first decisions was to implement the UNICEF principle that a Child Friendly City should produce a regular report to monitor the well-being of its children and young people (UNICEF 2011).

In 2010 the desire to create an indicator set was raised at a workshop run by the State Government Department of Education and Early Childhood Development (DEECD) to review Bendigo's Australian Early Development Index (AEDI) results (a national measure of children's development taken from all Australian children in their first year of school in 2009. A researcher from the Department of Planning and Community Development (DPCD) attended the workshop and offered St Luke's Anglicare a week's volunteering leave to write an indicator framework. At the completion of the volunteering leave, DEECD offered a small grant for a research assistant to be supervised to complete the data collection and for St Luke's Anglicare to publish the report.

A Community Owned Indicators Framework

Deciding what indicators to use is a critical decision for a community. Indicators highlight public policy issues and attention is drawn to issues with measures. If designed carefully indicators can become an effective and trusted public information source that can galvanise action and ensure policy is just (Salvaris and Wiseman 2004). If poorly designed, indicators risk being seen as a biased account of the issues communities face and ignored (Salvaris and Wiseman 2004). The first task of the indicator project was therefore to create an indicator framework that told the story about what was important to the community about its children and young people. Developing the framework began with a review of:

- the Leadership Group's strategic documents;
- a significant body of strategic and research work undertaken by the Local Government (City of Greater Bendigo) as part of its earlier child friendly commitment;
- State, Federal and international indicator frameworks; and
- the notes from the AEDI workshop.

During the review the developing framework was iterated with key stakeholders in interviews. The resulting framework is a statement that acknowledges that the well-being of children is dependent on the well-being of families (and vice versa) and that family well-being is in turn dependent on the well-being of communities (and vice versa). The framework statement reads: "In a child friendly city...

- Children are ... developing well; safe and secure; engaged learning and earning; happy and healthy; and active citizens;
- Families are ... providing a positive lifestyle; supported by child expertise; creating a positive learning environment, safe; modelling good citizenship; and
- Communities have... quality organisations, services and programs; capacity; quality infrastructure; broad networks; well planned, safe environments; community government and business working together; mechanisms for involving children's voices, and those working with children, in decision-making" (Pope and Nolan 2011).

The importance of writing the strategic story first—before looking at data—cannot be overstated. It ensured the story was not driven purely by available data and that important policy issues did not slip off the agenda simply because there are no measures. This was important when the Leadership Group came to select eight priority issues for action from the indicators, as half were data gaps. Once the framework was determined, data sources were reviewed for potential indicators in each topic area. To be included, indicators needed to come from a theoretically sound/ accepted and technically accurate time series data collection that described a topic at the Local Government Area level as a minimum. The draft framework, populated with forty potential indicators, was presented to a workshop of around forty stakeholders from Local and State government, the community sector, schools and academia. The workshop examined whether (i) the framework included all topics important to the community and (ii) the best indicators (including gaps) for each topic had been selected. To keep the story coherent, and focused on the issues of greatest importance, indicators were only allowed to be added if others were removed.

At the conclusion of the workshop, there was a very high level of agreement on both the overall framework and the indicators to populate it. This process created a locally relevant strategic story and ensured data gaps were identified.

The Final Report

The report was designed to compare each indicator for Bendigo to the state average using a simple traffic light graphic (green meaning Bendigo was doing better than the state average, orange same, red worse). Time trends were included if they were available. Detail was also given about when the next data would be available and how the community could find data for future reports. The report highlighted data gaps and noted if these would be filled by forthcoming data collections. The report also included summaries of one-off research projects in Bendigo that described aspects of children's well-being in more detail (such as research run by the City of Greater Bendigo into children's favourite places). Adding further research "case studies" in the future will build up a compendium of information about local children and young people's well-being over time. It has been important that funds were provided by DEECD to produce a high quality report for the community. It has also been important that the work of the community has been publicly acknowledged by significant people outside of the community. This has included a foreword by the Director of the Centre for Community Child Health, Frank Oberklaid, and the report being launched by well known children's rights advocate Moira Rainer and the State Minister for Children and Early Childhood Development, the Hon Wendy Lovell MLC. These endorsements added a sense of priority and commitment to the child friendly agenda.

Action Resulting from the Indicators: Strategic Planning and Building Support

The indicators have since been used for strategic planning and to build support and interest in partnership work. The Leadership Group has selected eight indicators as priorities, of which four are data gaps. Selection was made considering local energy/interest, key stakeholders existing strategic plans and budgeting opportunities. Creating priorities allows communities to focus on issues for which there is passion and enthusiasm and prevents them becoming overwhelmed by the enormity of complex problems that may take considerable time and effort to address. The Leadership Group presented the priority indicators to a workshop of its broader stakeholders to develop an action plan. Workshop participants were asked to reflect on how their work could positively impact the indicators and to specifically consider:

- How data gaps could be filled;
- The actions required to create improvements in the indicators; and
- Ways organisations could join up resources to progress action in these areas.

The Leadership Group has also agreed to take every opportunity to speak on the group's priorities and a *Communications and Community Engagement Strategy* is currently being written that includes explicit opportunities to raise awareness of the report to strengthen community ownership of Child Friendly City activities.

Indicator Projects as Triggers for Collaboration

The Bendigo Child Friendly City Leadership Group has created a high quality indicator report, *The State of Bendigo's Children* (Pope and Nolan 2011), that provides a snap shot of the well-being of children and young people living in Bendigo. The indicators populate an ecological framework that sees the well-being of children, their families and the community as interrelated. The creation of the indicators report has involved engagement of a wide range of local stakeholders. This has had the duel benefit of building local interest in, and ownership of, the Child Friendly Cities agenda and grounding its planned actions in the local policy and program environment. Stakeholders reported they enjoyed taking the time out from their regular work for a "big picture" strategic discussion about outcomes at the indicators workshops.

There were four reasons this project was a success. The first was the authorising environment and networks that initiated it. Bendigo had already built a network of individuals and organisations dedicated to this area of work. This meant there was a significant amount of community energy, support and assistance available when writing the report (particularly from the Local Government). Second, the Leadership Group used its broader networks to bring capacities and resources into the community that were not available locally. The relationship between the State government and the community in particular generated resources that made the project possible. Third, the engagement of a range of stakeholders throughout the project created a high quality report, fostered enthusiasm for the work and generated innovative ideas for future activities. Finally, the Leadership Group's networks have allowed local stakeholders to see interest in their work from a variety of influential people outside of the community, which has fostered continued motivation for the work. Overall, this project has worked because it brought together the three types of knowledge that underpin effective community planning: technical information, local knowledge and strategic/political knowledge (Salvaris and Wiseman 2004). Few organisations hold all three. Professor Fiona Stanley has described this as the "know-do gap" and argues it is an important barrier to overcome to improve the well-being of children and young people (in Bammer et al. 2010). Acting on the impact of Bendigo indicators demands this collaboration continues and is evident in not only the production and release of a second set of child-friendly Bendigo indicators in 2013 but for also stimulating a similar initiative in the neighbouring shire, Go Goldfields, a series of shire wide, community-driven approaches to improve social, education and health outcomes for children, youth and families.

Conclusion

There would appear to significant untapped potential for local children's well-being indicators reports to continue to stimulate innovation across children's services practice and research. However, the increasing resource constraints across most OECD countries is not only threatening to curtail some of the depth of national and local children's well-being reporting but also their capacity to be both implemented and evaluated. O'Hare (2008: 388) noted this in assessing the Kids Count Databook in the United States, that "[d]espite the proliferation of indicator-based efforts, however, little has been done to systematically assess the impact of these projects. A quick scan of several key books on child indicators shows virtually no coverage of impact assessment." Redmond (2012: 53) similarly laments that despite a 20 year increase in expenditure for Australian children from the mid-1980s to the mid-2000s, "a review of available indicators suggests that trends in Australian children's outcomes were not uniformly positive. In particular there is little substantive evidence that disparities in outcomes between children from lower and higher socio-economic backgrounds fell substantially."

In a complex system, there is no common approach to measuring the achievement of specific outcomes of individual organisations focused on child and youth well-being and this presents a barrier to demonstrating the aggregated contribution of the community sector to societal impact. However, a local state of children's report still provides a vital benchmark for tracking future progress and is an essential tool for ongoing community planning. It also allows services to coordinate responses around key areas that need further attention, promoting collaboration and partnership.

Acknowledgments This work was supported by the National Research Foundation of Korea Grant funded by the Korean Government (NRF-2013S1A3A2054622).

References

Abello, A., Gong, C. H., Daly, A., & McNamara, J. (2012). Spatial dimensions of child social exclusion risk in Australia: Widening the scope. *Child Indicators Research, 5,* 685–703.

Axford, N., Hobbs, T., & Jodrell, D. (2013). Making child well-being data work hard: Getting from data to policy and practice. *Child Indicators Research, 6,* 161–177.

Bammer, G., Michaux, A., & Sanson, A. (Eds.). (2010). *Bridging the "Know-Do" gap: Knowledge brokering to improve child well-being.* Canberra: Australian National University E Press.

Ben-Arieh, A. (2008). The child indicators movement: Past, present, and future. *Child Indicators Research, 1,* 3–16.

Ben-Arieh, A., & Goerge, R. (Eds.). (2006). *Indicators of children's well-being: Understanding their role, usage, and policy influence.* Dordrecht, The Netherlands: Springer.

Brown, B., & Moore, K. A. (2009). What gets measured gets done: High priority opportunities to improve our nation's capacity to monitor child and youth well-being. Annie E. Casey Foundation.

Coulton, C. J., Korbin, J. E., & McDonell, J. (2009). Editorial: Indicators of child well-being in the context of small areas. *Child Indicators Research, 2,* 109–110.

Fattore, T., Mason, J., & Watson, E. (2009). When children are asked about their well-being: Towards a framework for guiding policy. *Child Indicators Research, 2,* 57–77.

Hur, Y., & Testerman, R. (2012). An index of child well-being at a local level in the U.S.: The case of North Carolina counties. *Child Indicators Research, 5,* 29–53.

Klocke, A., Clair, A., & Bradshaw, J. (2014). International variation in child subjective well-being. *Child Indicators Research, 7,* 1–20.

Lau, M., & Bradshaw, J. (2010). Child well-being in the Pacific Rim. *Child Indicators Research, 3,* 367–383.

Moore, K. (1997). Criteria for indicators of child well-being. In R. Hauser, B. Brown, & W. Prosser (Eds.), *Indicators of children's well-being.* New York: Russell Sage Foundation.

Muir, K., Mullan, K., Powell, A., Flaxman, S., Thompson, D., & Griffiths, M. (2009). *State of Australia's young people: A report on the social, economic, health and family lives of young people*. Canberra: Department of Education, Employment and Workplace Relations and the Social Policy Research Centre, University of New South Wales.

O'Hare, W. P. (2008). Measuring the impact of child indicators. *Child Indicators Research, 1*, 387–396.

Pope, J., & Nolan, E. (2011). *State of Bendigo's children report*. St Luke's Anglicare: Bendigo. Available at: http://www.childfriendlycity.com.au/File.axd?id=a933f130-0c16-47d0-a473-2062dff69400. Accessed May 2014.

Redmond, G. (2012). Uncertain impacts: Trends in public expenditure on children and child outcomes in Australia since the 1980s. *Child Indicators Research, 5*, 753–770.

Salvaris, M., & Wiseman, J. (2004). *Mapping community well-being: Using community well-being indicators to choose goals and measure progress*. Carlton, Victoria: Victorian Health Promotion Foundation.

Sanson, A., Misson, S., Hawkins, M. T., & Berthelsen, D. (2010). The development and validation of Australian indices of child development—Part I: Conceptualisation and development. *Child Indicators Research, 3*, 275–292.

UNICEF. (2011). Child friendly cities website. Available at: http://www.childfriendlycities.org. Accessed May 2014.

UNICEF Office of Research. (2013). *Child well-being in rich countries: A comparative overview, Innocenti report card 11*. Florence: UNICEF Office of Research.

Chapter 5
Gender Equity and Community Well-Being

Sharan B. Merriam

Abstract Community well-being is a function of many factors working in concert to promote an optimal quality of life for all members of a community. It is argued here that attention to gender equity including the education and health of girls and women has a direct impact on numerous indicators of community well-being. Numerous international studies suggest that attention to gender equity creates human and social capital that enables community well-being. Human capital is the knowledge, skills and health embodied in individuals and social capital refers to the patterns and qualities of relationships in a community characterized by norms of trust and reciprocity. Women's education has been linked to a reduction in infant and childhood mortality, socio-economic development, community development, physical and mental well-being as well as other factors. Attention to gender equity and in particular girls and women's education, leads to greater human and social capital which in turn leads to community well-being.

Keywords Social capital · Women's education · Gender equity · Empowerment

Defining and Assessing Community Well-Being

Community well-being is a complex concept that refers to an optimal quality of life for people living together in communities. It matters little if we are talking about a small rural village in a remote part of an African country or a high-tech city of skyscrapers in the busiest urban areas of Asia. Industrialization, technological sophistication, and economic development, while improving the lives of many, do not in and of themselves insure for community well-being. Take the small Asian country of Bhutan, for example. By any economic measure, this tiny rural

S.B. Merriam (✉)
University of Georgia, Athens, USA
e-mail: smerriam@uga.edu

© Springer International Publishing Switzerland 2016
Y. Kee et al. (eds.), *Social Factors and Community Well-Being*,
SpringerBriefs in Well-Being and Quality of Life Research,
DOI 10.1007/978-3-319-29942-6_5

country would be classified as a developing nation. Bhutan however, uses Gross National Happiness (GNH) versus Gross Domestic Product (GDP) as the country's measure of well-being and development.

The complexity of assessing community well-being is further underscored by a recently released report titled *Social Progress Index* (Porter and Stern 2014). Social progress is defined as "the capacity of a society to meet the basic human needs of its citizens, establish the building blocks that allow citizens and communities to enhance and sustain the quality of their lives, and create the conditions for all individuals to reach their full potential" (p. 7). A country's well-being is assessed by looking at three general factors, (1) *basic human needs* including nutrition, water, shelter and safety, (2) *foundations of well-being* which include access to basic knowledge, information, and communication, health and wellness, ecosystem sustainability, and (3) *opportunity* involving personal freedom, choice and rights, tolerance and inclusion, and access to advanced education. The most socially progressive country out of 132 countries is New Zealand, followed by Switzerland, and Iceland. The rankings of the 132 countries can be found in Porter and Stern's 2014 report. It is interesting to note that high per capita GDP does not necessarily equate to a high social progress rating, lending more support to the argument that well-being consists of more than economic measures.

Another international study, The World Happiness Report (2013), rated 156 countries on happiness scores and found that "people who are emotionally happier, who have more satisfying lives, and who live in happier communities, are more likely both now and later to be healthy, productive, and socially connected. These benefits in turn flow more broadly to their families, workplaces and communities, to the advantage of all" (p. 4). The top five countries are Denmark, Norway, Switzerland, Netherlands, and Sweden.

Clearly, community well-being is a function of numerous variables, many of which are difficult to measure and many of which can only be assessed indirectly. For example, Merriam and Kee (2014) make the case that promoting lifelong learning among older adults can significantly contribute to community well-being. They found that "there is ample evidence, both anecdotal and research based, that learning in older adulthood not only reduces dependency on government-funded social services but actually enhances personal and community wellbeing" (p. 133). In a similar vein, it is argued in this paper that promoting gender equity including the education and health of girls and women has a direct impact on numerous indicators of community well-being. Promoting gender equity leads to increases in human and social capital thus enhancing community well-being.

Human and Social Capital

Efforts to promote and/or assess community wellbeing require identifying factors associated with an optimal quality of life for people living together in communities. Different forms of capital (assets or resources) offers one such theoretical framework. Capital is most often thought of in economic and particularly monetary terms but Bourdieu (1986) extended the idea of capital to include three forms: economic capital, cultural capital and social capital. He defines social capital as "the aggregate of the actual or potential resources which are linked to possession of a durable network of more or less institutionalized relationships of mutual acquaintance and recognition." In a well-known exploration of the link between social capital and personal and community well-being, Putnam (2000) traces the ebb and flow of social capital in American society. He laments that as we have become increasingly disconnected from family, friends, neighbors and social structures, there is a loss of social capital that is a serious threat to our civic and personal health. Further, "communities with less social capital have lower educational performance and more teen pregnancy, child suicide, low birth weight, and prenatal mortality. Social capital is also a strong predictor of crime rates and other measures of neighborhood quality of life, as it is of our health" (inside dust jacket).

There are now many frameworks differentiating different types of capital. One such framework proposed by Black and Hughes (2001) is particularly helpful in looking at community wellbeing. They propose four different types of capital: (1) natural capital consists of natural resources and the ecosystem that defines a geographic space; (2) economic capital includes the products, the physical infrastructure, and financial resources; (3) human capital is the knowledge, skills, and health embodied in individuals and (4) social capital refers to the interactions, networks, and patterns of relationships among people in a community. In this paper I argue that attending to gender equity directly promotes both human and social capital which in turn relate to community wellbeing.

Gender Equity

As noted above, community wellbeing is a function of a cluster of factors that come together, synergistically affecting a community as a whole. As new, massively built but abandoned cities and shopping malls in China suggest (Miklos 2013), infrastructure is certainly one factor, but infrastructure itself is not enough to create a community, let alone enhance a community's wellbeing. Natural resources are also important but again resource-rich communities are not necessarily better off than resource-poor communities. What does seem to make a difference are human factors, the health and well-being of people who reside in a particular community. *It is argued here that community well-being can be enhanced by equalizing women's access to resources and opportunities in all spheres of community life.* The evidence is overwhelming—the lower status of women in society constitutes a handicap to community well-being affecting men as well as women. As Carter (2014) writes in his recent book, *A Call to Action; Women, Religion, Violence, and Power* "prejudice, discrimination, war, violence, distorted interpretations of religious texts, physical and mental abuse, poverty, and disease fall disproportionately on women and girls" (p. 1). Further, Carter has come to feel that *"the most serious and unaddressed worldwide challenge is the deprivation and abuse of women and girls"* which has "a devastating effect on economic prosperity" which is not "just a women's issue" and "It is not confined to the poorest countries. It affects us all" (p. 3, italics in original). Gender equity is about fairness in the way women and men are treated. That is not to say that women are given preferential treatment. Rather, the different life experiences and needs of men and women are taken into consideration and attention in the form of some sort of compensation is made for women's historical and social disadvantages. *Gender equity* thus serves to level the playing field and positions women to be able to access opportunities that have historically favored men. Therefore, we can say that equity is essential to achieving true equality.

Several major international studies offer support for the linkage between gender equity and by extension, community well-being. Probably the best known of these studies is the annual report from the World Economic Forum on the Status of Women in 132 countries (http://www3.weforum.org/docs/WEF_GenderGap_Report_2013.pdf). Each country is assessed on four indicators: (1) women's education, (2) women's health and life expectancy, (3) socio-economic status, and (4) political power. The first measure, women's education, is captured through ratios of women to men in primary-, secondary- and tertiary-level education. A longer-term view of the country's ability to educate women and men in equal numbers is captured through the ratio of the female literacy rate to the male literacy rate. Health and life expectancy are assessed through two measures, sex-ratio at birth and the gap between women's and men's healthy life expectancy, calculated by the World Health Organization. "This measure provides an estimate of the number of years that women and men can expect to live in good health by taking into account the years lost to violence, disease, malnutrition or other relevant factors" (p. 4). Socio-economic status is assessed through several measures of the difference in labor force participation rates. Finally, political power measures "the gap between men and women at the highest level of political decision-making, through the ratio of women to men in minister-level positions and the ratio of women to men in parliamentary positions. In addition, we include the ratio of women to men in terms of years in executive office (prime minister or president) for the last 50 years" (p. 4).

For 2013, the five top ranked countries were Iceland, Finland, Norway, Sweden and the Philippines. It is also interesting to note that several top-ranked countries on gender equity are also top rated in the World Happiness Report and the recent Social Progress Index (see above). Appendix A is a table of the rankings of all 132 countries. Again, it is interesting to note that no single measure results in a higher ranking. The small African country of Lesotho at #16 outranks the United States ranked at #23. Romania (#70) and Honduras (#82) outrank both Japan (#105) and Korea (#111). This study suggests that much work needs to be done worldwide to ensure for gender equity and by extension, community well-being.

A second major international report, the OECD's Better Life Index, assesses "well-being" in 36 developed countries. The top ten ranked countries are Australia, Sweden, Canada, Norway, Switzerland, United States, Denmark, Netherlands, Iceland and the United Kingdom. Well-being is measured in two domains, material living conditions and quality of life. Material living conditions consists of three measures—income and wealth, jobs and earnings, and housing conditions. Quality of life is assessed by measuring eight variables—health status, work-life balance, education and skills, social connections, civic engagement and governance, environmental quality, personal security and subjective well-being. These eight variables assessing quality of life are measures of human and social capital. The authors devote an entire chapter in the report to gender differences in well-being. Men's and women's responses are evaluated on each of the eleven measures listed above. They conclude:

> While traditional disadvantages faced by women and girls persist in most countries, men and boys are increasingly exposed to uncertain job prospects and need to adapt to changing tasks and social expectations. Although men continue to score higher than women in a number of areas, no gender consistently outperforms the other and the gender gaps in well-being have been narrowing in recent decades. Whilst women live longer than men they are also ill more often. Girls are doing better than boys in school but still remain underrepresented in the key fields of education that provide greater job opportunities. Similarly, while women are increasingly present in the labour market, they still earn less than men, spend more hours in unpaid work and find it harder to reach the top of the career ladder or start their own business. Men are more often the victims of homicide and assault, but women are the primary target of intimate partner violence. Finally, although women are more satisfied with their lives than men, they are more likely to experience negative emotions (OECD 2013, p. 103).

And congruent with the above studies, the World Happiness Report mentioned earlier found that for those countries with the highest ratings, gender equity is a national priority. Not surprisingly, women are relatively happier in countries where gender rights are more equal (Graham and Chattopadhyay 2011).

Women's Empowerment, Education, and Community Well-Being

The link between gender equity and community well-being seems well-supported by the several major international studies cited above. Countries that rank high on the status of women are among the same countries that rank in the top tier of world happiness, OECD's Better Life Index assessing "well-being," and the most recent report, the Social Progress Index which assessed the social progress of 132 countries. In addition there are dozens of studies that support the link between attention to women's issues and specific measures of community well-being. For example, there is a well-supported connection between women's literacy at even the most basic level, and a reduction in infant and childhood mortality. Infant mortality and its strong association with women's empowerment has been used worldwide as proxy measure of community well-being:

> Gender empowerment is also shown to be highly correlated with infant mortality. One study (Varkey, et al.) found that scores on national Gender Empowerment Measures (GEMs) were strongly correlated with variables that measure the health of communities,

including low birth weight and fertility. But the strongest association was between gender empowerment and infant mortality. An Egyptian study found that key aspects of women's empowerment, including "lifetime exposure to employment" and "family structure amenable to empowerment" (positively) and "traditional marriage (negatively) were strongly related to child survival (Kishor). (Casper and Simmons 2013, p. 96)

Likewise, women's education is key to reducing maternal mortality (McAlister and Baskett 2006). Attention to female education at all levels has resulted in reduced birth rates and subsequent rise in economic living standards in many countries. In these countries women no longer feel it necessary to have many children to insure a few survive to aid in a family's income and caretaking later in life; the better educated woman herself can find employment and afford to raise a few healthy children. A lower birth rate has been associated with a country's economic progress to the point that a few countries are growing concerned that the birth rate is below the population replacement rate!

Indeed, learning and education seems to be a good place to begin addressing both female equity and community well-being. In fact in repressive societies, the education of girls and women is seen as a direct threat to maintaining brutal, male-dominated social systems. Malala Yousafzai, the Pakistani young teen who survived a gunshot in the head by Taliban for going to school and advocating education for girls, has become a worldwide symbol and advocate of the power of education to change girls and women's status in the world. Likewise, the recent kidnapping of the best and brightest schoolgirls in Nigeria by the terrorist group Boko Haram (meaning Western education is forbidden) further underscores the power and hence threat of education for females. In a report on the relationship between well-being and education in Western society, Field (2009) writes, "the evidence that learning promotes well-being is overwhelming" (p. 5) and well-being is a form of human and social capital:

> Well-being…is a dynamic state, in which the individual is able to develop their potential, work productively and creatively, build strong and positive relationships with others and contribute to their community. It is enhanced when an individual is able to fulfill their personal and social goals and achieve a sense of purpose in society. In policy terms, it can be defined as the conditions which allow individuals and communities to flourish (p. 9).

Further, "well-being is also associated with better health, higher levels of social and civic engagement, and greater resilience in the face of external crises. So if adult learning already affects people's life changes directly, it can also affect them indirectly by enhancing their well-being" (Field 2009, p. 14).

The Challenge of Promoting and Assessing the Link Between Gender Equity and Community Well-Being

All of the international assessments of well-being, social progress, happiness and status of women and smaller scale research studies on particular issues such as infant mortality all confirm that the link between gender equity and more specifically women's empowerment and community well-being is indisputable. The challenge is how to assess progress in gender equity especially given the vast cultural, historical, and economic disparities across the world. The United Nations' Millennium Development Goals is one overarching framework for considering this challenge. At the Millennium Summit meeting in 2003, all members of the United Nations committed to achieving eight development goals by 2015. These eight goals are as follows:

1. To eradicate extreme poverty and hunger
2. To achieve universal primary education
3. To promote gender equality and empower women
4. To reduce child mortality
5. To improve maternal health
6. To combat HIV/AIDS, malaria, and other diseases
7. To ensure environmental sustainability
8. To develop a global partnership for development.

In addition to goal three, "to promote gender equality and empower women," several of the other goals disproportionately affect girls and women (access to primary education, child mortality and maternal health). There are also specific goals under each of the eight development goals. For goal three, the sub-goals are:

- Gender inequality slows development. Equal political, economic, social and cultural rights are required to reduce poverty.
- Women's ability to decide freely the number and timing of children is key to their empowerment and expanded opportunities for work, education and social participation.
- Men play a pivotal role in achieving gender equality, poverty reduction and development goals, including improved infant and maternal health and reduced HIV transmission and gender-based violence.
- Violence against women and girls results in high social and economic costs-to individuals, families and public budgets.
- Eliminating child marriage, enabling adolescent girls to delay pregnancy, ending discrimination against pregnant girls, and providing support to young mothers can help ensure that girls complete an education. This can help break the cycle of intergenerational poverty.
- Girls' secondary education provides high payoffs for poverty reduction, gender equality, labour force participation and reproductive health, including HIV prevention and women's and children's health and education status overall.

As might be expected, progress toward these goals has been uneven and somewhat dependent upon the specificity of the goal and thus its measurability. For example, HIV/AIDS and malaria eradication has seen some progress as has the promotion of universal primary education. Gender equality and empowering women is harder to assess although the World Economic Forum's annual Status of Women report does an admirable job of tracking changes in four measures of women's equity. Speaking of the MDGs and their impact on issues of women's equity: "The conclusions of the experts are clear: Investing in gender equality, reproductive health and young people's development has short- and long-term social and economic multiplier effects. Launching national campaigns on violence against women; promoting women's property and inheritance rights; expanding access to reproductive health care and closing funding gaps for supplies and contraceptives; and ensuring that women are involved in the formulation of MDG follow-up policies and strategies are among the high-impact "quick wins" identified by the UN Millennium Project" (http://vcampus.uom.ac.mu/socil101/434_the_mdgs_linkages_fo_poverty_reduction-gender-equality_and_reproductive_health.html).

Finally, Malhotra and Schuler (2005) have grappled with the issues involved in measuring women's empowerment. After reviewing dozens of studies from several disciplines they proposed a framework for developing empowerment indicators. Their framework consists of five dimensions (economic, social and cultural, legal, political and psychological) of women's empowerment across three domains (household, community, broader areas). For example, under the social and cultural dimension, women's empowerment would mean that girls in a family have equal access to education (household), that later marriage and self-selection of spouses be accepted (community), and that females have access to a broad range of educational options, and to health systems (broader areas). This framework presents both the complexity of assessing progress in this area as well as identifying specific variables that can be assessed to measure progress in women's empowerment.

In summary, a strong case can be made that the well-being of a community is directly linked to girls and women having the same access to a society's opportunities as do boys and men. International studies of happiness, social progress, well-being, and the status of women all suggest that the status of women needs to be raised to match that of men. Then equal treatment will have equal results, but as long as women are lower status and lag behind, equal treatment won't get equal results. Smaller scale studies of specific wellness indicators such as infant mortality, women's health, access to education, employment, and governance all come to the same conclusion—that a community is better off when girls and women are treated the same as men. Equal opportunity and access build human and social capital; both forms of capital serve to strengthen our communities and strong communities are the building blocks of prosperous and peaceful societies.

Appendix A

(See Table A.1).

Table A.1 Detailed rankings, 2013

Country	Overall		Economic participation and opportunity		Educational attainment		Health and survival		Political empowerment	
	Rank	Score	Rank	Score	Rank	Score	Rank	Score	Rank	Score
Iceland	1	0.8731	22	0.7684	1	1.0000	97	0.9696	1	0.7544
Finland	2	0.8421	19	0.7727	1	1.0000	1	0.9796	2	0.6162
Norway	3	0.8417	1	0.8357	1	1.0000	93	0.9697	3	0.5616
Sweden	4	0.8129	14	0.7829	38	0.9977	69	0.9735	4	0.4976
Philippines	5	0.7832	16	0.7773	1	1.0000	1	0.9796	10	0.3760
Ireland	6	0.7823	29	0.7450	34	0.9988	65	0.9737	6	0.4115
New Zealand	7	0.7799	15	0.7797	1	1.0000	93	0.9697	12	0.3703
Denmark	8	0.7779	25	0.7639	1	1.0000	64	0.9739	11	0.3738
Switzerland	9	0.7736	23	0.7681	66	0.9919	72	0.9733	16	0.3610
Nicaragua	10	0.7715	91	0.6218	28	0.9996	55	0.9758	5	0.4889
Belgium	11	0.7684	34	0.7367	67	0.9918	47	0.9787	14	0.3664
Latvia	12	0.7610	17	0.7767	1	1.0000	1	0.9796	26	0.2875
Netherlands	13	0.7608	26	0.7592	44	0.9954	93	0.9697	22	0.3191
Germany	14	0.7583	46	0.7120	86	0.9818	49	0.9780	15	0.3611
Cuba	15	0.7540	65	0.6736	30	0.9995	63	0.9743	13	0.3685
Lesotho	16	0.7530	18	0.7756	1	1.0000	1	0.9796	35	0.2570
South Africa	17	0.7510	78	0.6505	54	0.9941	102	0.9677	3	0.3919
United Kingdom	18	0.7440	35	0.7320	31	0.9994	92	0.9698	29	0.2747
Austria	19	0.7437	69	0.6642	1	1.0000	47	0.9787	19	0.3318
Canada	20	0.7425	9	0.7959	1	1.0000	49	0.9780	42	0.1959
Luxembourg	21	0.7410	7	0.8162	1	1.0000	85	0.9719	51	0.1757
Burundi	22	0.7397	3	0.8307	114	0.8895	99	0.9685	31	0.2702
United States	23	0.7392	6	0.8185	1	1.0000	33	0.9792	60	0.1593

(continued)

Table A.1 (continued)

Country	Overall		Economic participation and opportunity		Educational attainment		Health and survival		Political empowerment	
	Rank	Score	Rank	Score	Rank	Score	Rank	Score	Rank	Score
Australia	24	0.7390	13	0.7879	1	1.0000	69	0.9735	43	0.1945
Ecuador	25	0.7389	90	0.6253	52	0.9942	55	0.9758	17	0.3604
Mozambique	26	0.7349	11	0.7897	124	0.8355	112	0.9612	18	0.3533
Bolivia	27	0.7340	57	0.6841	99	0.9623	84	0.9719	23	0.3175
Lithuania	28	0.7308	21	0.7688	60	0.9928	34	0.9791	47	0.1826
Barbados	29	0.7301	10	0.7907	1	1.0000	1	0.9796	63	0.1503
Spain	30	0.7266	76	0.6521	40	0.9971	75	0.9730	27	0.2841
Costa Rica	31	0.7241	98	0.5955	1	1.0000	62	0.9747	21	0.3263
Kazakhstan	32	0.7218	20	0.7706	69	0.9913	1	0.9796	65	0.1458
Mongolia	33	0.7204	2	0.8338	49	0.9946	1	0.9796	108	0.0734
Argentina	34	0.7195	101	0.5887	42	0.9962	1	0.9796	24	0.3136
Colombia	35	0.7171	39	0.7275	45	0.9954	34	0.9791	55	0.1662
Trinidad and Tobago	36	0.7166	47	0.7112	51	0.9944	130	0.9516	38	0.2092
Panama	37	0.7164	45	0.7136	43	0.9958	61	6.9753	48	0.1811
Slovenia	38	0.7155	43	0.7189	26	0.9999	75	0.9730	54	0.1702
Malawi	39	0.7139	4	0.8253	112	0.8961	101	0.9683	56	0.1660
Bahamas	40	0.7128	5	0.8244	1	1.0000	1	0.9796	124	0.0471
Cape Verde	41	0.7122	96	0.6020	97	0.9663	1	0.9796	25	0.3011
Serbia	42	0.7116	59	0.6791	55	0.9940	111	0.9642	39	0.2089
Bulgaria	43	0.7097	49	0.7067	64	0.9924	34	0.9791	58	0.1606
Namibia	44	0.7094	53	0.6980	1	1.0000	105	0.9671	52	0.1727
France	45	0.7089	67	0.6690	1	1.0000	1	0.9796	45	0.1870
Uganda	46	0.7086	37	0.7285	123	0.8425	1	0.9796	28	0.2839

(continued)

Table A.1 (continued)

Country	Overall		Economic participation and opportunity		Educational attainment		Health and survival		Political empowerment	
	Rank	Score	Rank	Score	Rank	Score	Rank	Score	Rank	Score
Jamaica	47	0.7085	36	0.7317	80	0.9884	1	0.9796	74	0.1345
Guyana	48	0.7085	102	0.5885	1	1.0000	45	0.9789	33	0.2668
Croatia	49	0.7069	61	0.6753	47	0.9951	34	0.9791	50	0.1779
Venezuela	50	0.7060	89	0.6256	33	0.9993	1	0.9796	37	0.2196
Portugal	51	0.7056	66	0.6726	56	0.9940	83	0.9724	46	0.1834
Moldova	52	0.7037	32	0.7407	74	0.9907	34	0.9791	87	0.1043
Israel	53	0.7032	56	0.6915	82	0.9874	93	0.9697	57	0.1643
Poland	54	0.7031	73	0.6563	37	0.9983	34	0.9791	49	0.1786
Sri Lanka	55	0.7019	109	0.5590	48	0.9946	1	0.9796	30	0.2744
Madagascar	56	0.7016	51	0.7033	93	0.9750	74	0.9732	61	0.1547
Macedonia	57	0.7013	71	0.6611	75	0.9903	128	0.9533	40	0.2007
Singapore	58	0.7000	12	0.7883	105	0.9409	85	0.9719	90	0.0989
Estonia	59	0.6997	41	0.7228	59	0.9931	34	0.9791	88	0.1038
Lao PDA*	60	0.6993	8	0.7999	113	0.8948	106	0.9669	73	0.1355
Russian Federation	61	0.6983	42	0.7204	36	0.9984	34	0.9791	94	0.0951
Brazil	62	0.6949	74	0.6561	1	1.0000	1	0.9796	68	0.1440
Kyrgyz Republic	63	0.6948	60	0.6789	77	0.9888	75	0.9730	71	0.1383
Ukraine	64	0.6935	30	0.7426	27	0.9998	75	0.9730	119	0.0587
Thailand	65	0.6928	50	0.7035	78	0.9888	1	0.9796	89	0.0992
Tanzania	66	0.6928	70	0.6635	118	0.8779	112	0.9612	32	0.2684
Senegal	67	0.6923	81	0.6401	125	0.8270	71	0.9734	20	0.3286
Mexico	68	0.6917	111	0.5499	70	0.9911	1	0.9796	36	0.2463
China	69	0.6908	62	0.6752	81	0.9880	133	0.9398	59	0.1604

(continued)

Table A.1 (continued)

Country	Overall		Economic participation and opportunity		Educational attainment		Health and survival		Political empowerment	
	Rank	Score	Rank	Score	Rank	Score	Rank	Score	Rank	Score
Romania	70	0.6908	55	0.6928	50	0.9945	34	0.9791	91	0.0970
Italy	71	0.6885	97	0.5973	65	0.9924	72	0.9733	44	0.1912
Dominican Republic	72	0.6867	63	0.6751	84	0.9822	89	0.9711	84	0.1184
Vietnam	73	0.6863	52	0.7023	95	0.9741	132	0.9441	80	0.1247
Slovak Republic	74	0.6857	86	0.6350	1	1.0000	1	0.9796	77	0.1284
Bangladesh	75	0.6848	121	0.4954	115	0.8846	124	0.9557	7	0.4036
Ghana	76	0.6811	24	0.7662	111	0.8970	104	0.9674	95	0.0937
Uruguay	77	0.6803	58	0.6833	41	0.9967	1	0.9796	116	0.0617
Kenya	78	0.6803	44	0.7146	107	0.9230	102	0.9677	85	0.1157
Cyprus	79	0.6801	85	0.6353	83	0.9853	91	0.9701	76	0.1298
Peru	80	0.6787	88	0.6278	88	0.9796	109	0.9658	69	0.1417
Greece	81	0.6782	79	0.6470	46	0.9953	65	0.9737	92	0.0969
Honduras	82	0.6773	94	0.6061	35	0.9988	52	0.9762	78	0.1280
Czech Republic	83	0.6770	95	0.6039	1	1.0000	46	0.9788	79	0.1254
Malta	84	0.6761	108	0.5655	58	0.9935	65	0.9737	53	0.1716
Botswana	85	0.6752	48	0.7108	1	1.0000	127	0.9549	127	0.0353
Georgia	86	0.6750	64	0.6741	89	0.9790	126	0.9553	97	0.0915
Hungary	87	0.6742	68	0.6677	62	0.9925	34	0.9791	120	0.0574
Brunei Darussalam	88	0.6730	33	0.7372	76	0.9889	109	0.9658	135	0.0000
Paraguay	89	0.6724	83	0.6363	61	0.9928	55	0.9758	104	0.0847
Tajikistan	90	0.6682	38	0.7284	110	0.8993	123	0.9559	100	0.0891
Chile	91	0.6670	112	0.5445	32	0.9993	1	0.9796	67	0.1448
Angola*	92	0.6659	92	0.6163	127	0.8062	1	0.9796	34	0.2614

(continued)

Table A.1 (continued)

Country	Overall		Economic participation and opportunity		Educational attainment		Health and survival		Political empowerment	
	Rank	Score	Rank	Score	Rank	Score	Rank	Score	Rank	Score
Bhutan*	93	0.6651	27	0.7528	116	0.8843	82	0.9725	122	0.0509
Armenia	94	0.6634	82	0.6384	29	0.9995	131	0.9497	115	0.0662
Indonesia	95	0.6613	103	0.5881	101	0.9574	107	0.9663	75	0.1334
El Salvador	96	0.6609	114	0.5345	79	0.9886	1	0.9796	70	0.1409
Maldives	97	0.6604	99	0.5914	1	1.0000	112	0.9612	101	0.0890
Mauritius	98	0.6599	105	0.5735	72	0.9907	1	0.9796	93	0.0959
Azerbaijan	99	0.6582	72	0.6591	85	0.9820	136	0.9254	114	0.0663
Cameroon	100	0.6560	40	0.7258	122	0.8470	112	0.9612	99	0.0902
India	101	0.6551	124	0.4465	120	0.8574	135	0.9312	9	0.3852
Malaysia	102	0.6518	100	0.5904	73	0.9907	75	0.9730	121	0.0530
Burkina Faso	103	0.6513	28	0.7467	128	0.7987	99	0.9685	98	0.0914
Cambodia	104	0.6509	77	0.6514	117	0.8811	1	0.9796	96	0.0916
Japan	105	0.6498	104	0.5841	91	0.9757	34	0.9791	118	0.0603
Nigeria	106	0.6469	54	0.6965	126	0.8115	122	0.9607	83	0.1190
Belize	107	0.6449	80	0.6458	103	0.9445	1	0.9796	133	0.0099
Albania	108	0.6412	87	0.6324	92	0.9755	134	0.9313	130	0.0256
United Arab Emirates	109	0.6372	122	0.4672	1	1.0000	112	0.9612	81	0.1206
Suriname	110	0.6369	119	0.4986	39	0.9973	1	0.9796	110	0.0723
Korea, Rep.	111	0.6351	118	0.5036	100	0.9592	75	0.9730	86	0.1046
Bahrain	112	0.6334	117	0.5146	71	0.9911	112	0.9612	113	0.0667
Zambia	113	0.6312	84	0.6354	121	0.8472	98	0.9690	109	0.0732
Guatemala	114	0.6304	113	0.5422	102	0.9522	1	0.9796	123	0.0475
Qatar	115	0.6299	106	0.5735	53	0.9941	129	0.9522	135	0.0000

(continued)

Table A.1 (continued)

Country	Overall		Economic participation and opportunity		Educational attainment		Health and survival		Political empowerment	
	Rank	Score	Rank	Score	Rank	Score	Rank	Score	Rank	Score
Kuwait	116	0.6292	115	0.5252	57	0.9936	112	0.9612	126	0.0370
Fiji	117	0.6286	120	0.4975	63	0.9925	1	0.9796	125	0.0448
Ethiopia	118	0.6198	93	0.6148	131	0.7451	68	0.9737	66	0.1457
Jordan	119	0.6093	128	0.4145	68	0.9915	90	0.9706	117	0.0607
Turkey	120	0.6081	127	0.4269	104	0.9431	59	0.9755	103	0.0868
Nepal	121	0.6053	116	0.5151	130	0.7462	112	0.9612	41	0.1989
Oman	122	0.6053	123	0.4489	94	0.9745	59	0.9755	132	0.0221
Lebanon	123	0.6028	126	0.4420	87	0.9796	1	0.9796	133	0.0099
Algeria	124	0.5966	133	0.3307	106	0.9387	108	0.9661	62	0.1511
Egypt	125	0.5935	125	0.4426	108	0.9199	51	0.9768	128	0.0348
Benin	126	0.5885	31	0.7419	136	0.5127	112	0.9612	72	0.1383
Saudi Arabia	127	0.5879	134	0.3223	90	0.9761	52	0.9762	105	0.0769
Mali	128	0.5872	107	0.5668	132	0.7291	54	0.9761	106	0.0769
Morocco	129	0.5845	129	0.3949	109	0.9002	88	0.9712	111	0.0720
Iran. Islamic Rep.	130	0.5842	130	0.3655	98	0.9653	87	0.9714	129	0.0346
Côte d'Ivoire	131	0.5814	110	0.5561	133	0.7141	1	0.9796	107	0.0758
Mauritania	132	0.5810	131	0.3651	119	0.8591	1	0.9796	82	0.1201
Syria	133	0.5661	136	0.2508	96	0.9682	58	0.9756	112	0.0697
Chad	134	0.5588	75	0.6547	135	0.5311	112	0.9612	102	0.0883
Pakistan	135	0.5459	135	0.3108	129	0.7685	124	0.9557	64	0.1487
Yemen	136	0.5128	132	0.3577	134	0.6980	81	0.9727	131	0.0227

Acknowledgments This chapter was presented at the 3rd international Forum on Community Well-being on June 23rd, 2015 at the Hoam Faculty House, Seoul, South Korea and was supported by the National Research Foundation of Korea Grant funded by the Korean Government (NRF-2013S1A3A2054622).

References

Black, A., & Hughes P. (2001). The identification and analysis of indicators of community strength and outcomes. Commonwealth Department of Family and Community Services, AU Bureau of Statistics. Retrieved May 20, 2014 from http://www.dss.gov.au/sites/default/files/documents/052012/no.3.pdf.

Bourdieu, P. (1986). The forms of capital. In J. Richardson (Ed.), *Handbook of theory and research for the sociology of education* (pp. 241–258). New York: Greenwood.

Carter, J. (2014). *A call to action: Women, religion, violence, and power.* New York: Simon & Schuster.

Casper, M. J., & Simmons, W. P. (2013). Accounting for death: Infant mortality, the MDGs, and women's (dis)empowerment. In *Counting on Marilyn earing: New advances in feminist economics.* Bradford, ON: Demeter Press. Retrieved May 28, 2014 from http://www.books.google.com.

Field, J. (2009). *Well-being and happiness: Inquiry into the future of lifelong learning* (Thematic paper 4). Leicester, UK: National Institute of Adult Continuing Education. Retrieved May 27, 2014 from http://www.academia.edu/25550251/Well-being_and_happiness.

Graham, C., & Chattopadhyay, S. (2011). *Gender and well-being around the world: Some insights from the economics of happiness.* Mimeo: The Brookings Institute.

Malhotra, A., & Schuler, S. R. (2005). Women's empowerment as a variable in international development. In D. Narayan (Ed.), *Measuring empowerment: Cross-disciplinary perspectives.* Washington, D.C: The World Bank.

McAlister, C., & Baskett, T. F. (2006). Female education and maternal mortality: A worldwide survey. *Journal of Obstetrics and Gynaecological Cancer, 28*(11), 983–990.

Merriam, S. B., & Kee, Y. (2014). Promoting community well-being: The case for lifelong learning for older adults. *Adult Education Quarterly, 64*(2), 128–144.

Miklos, V. (2013). China's brand-new abandoned cities could be dystopian movie sets. Retrieved April 17, 2014 from http://io9.com/chinas-brand-new-abandoned-cities-could-be-dystopian-m-1238731420.

OECD. (2013). *How's life? 2013: Measuring well-being.* France: OECD Publishing.

Porter, M. E., Stern, S., & Green, M. (2014). *Social progress index 2014: Executive summary.* Social progress imperative. Retrieved April 23, 2014 from http://www.skollfoundation.org/wp-content/uploads/2013/09/Exec-Summary-SPI.pdf.

Putnam, R. D. (2000). *Bowling alone: The collapse and revival of American community.* New York: Simon & Schuster.

World Happiness Report. (2013). Retrieved May 2, 2014 from http://unsdsn.org/resources/publications/world-happiness-report-2013/.

Chapter 6
Crime and Community Well-Being: The Role of Social Capital and Collective Efficacy in Increasing Safety

David C. Sloane and Hyunsun Choi

Abstract Safety plays a central role in individual and community well-being. Scholars have long examined an individual's perception of their safety (subjective well-being) and the reality of crime (objective well-being) in their cities and towns. Here, we examine the role that safety has in affecting a community's sense of well-being at a neighborhood scale. Positive community development requires that a neighborhood be safe. Improving safety is not just a role for the police and other governmental agencies. Instead, residents are important, even primary creators of safe neighborhoods in partnership with the criminal justice system. Critical to developing strong community actions to sustain safety are two relatively new concepts in sociology, criminology, and urban planning: social capital and collective efficacy. We discuss the role these concepts play in increasing a community's sense of well-being through networking and connectivity, which leads to increased safety and happiness.

Keywords Neighborhood safety · Social capital · Collective efficacy · Community well-being

Safety plays a central role in community well-being (CWB). As Rath et al. (2010: 93–4) remind us, "Community Well-being starts with the basics ... Feeling safe walking alone at night in your neighborhood and having confidence you wouldn't be harmed or assaulted is [a] primary necessity." They go on, "In countries around the world ... millions of people report they do not have this security. Even in the United States, United Kingdom, France, Germany, and [other] parts of Western Europe and Australia, as many as one in three people don't feel safe walking alone at night where they live." And, the percentage is often much higher in less

D.C. Sloane (✉)
Price School of Public Policy, University of Southern California, Los Angeles, USA

H. Choi
Department of Public Administration, Myong-Ji University, Seoul, South Korea

© Springer International Publishing Switzerland 2016   87
Y. Kee et al. (eds.), *Social Factors and Community Well-Being*,
SpringerBriefs in Well-Being and Quality of Life Research,
DOI 10.1007/978-3-319-29942-6_6

developed countries. Community members who do not feel safe are much less likely to feel happy or to be able to access neighborhood resources, such as parks, that would allow them to feel connected to their neighbors.

Unsafe places are difficult places for people to live and prosper because they constantly feel stressed by the fear of something happening to them or their family members. As a result, they often take actions that heighten their isolation—such as erecting gates around their house, putting bars on their windows, and keeping their children inside to play (Cozes and Davies 2013). In a neighborhood with higher community well-being, residents have a greater sense of spatial freedom since they can travel to parks, grocery stores, restaurants, friends' houses, and other spaces where they reconnect on a daily basis with their neighbors.

Ironically, that freedom to connect actually reinforces itself since by talking with a neighbor at the hardware store or sitting with a group in the park, residents increase the community's safety and well-being. They create a virtuous spiral where acts of neighborliness create more safety, thus feeling safer leads to more acts of neighborliness, allowing for the community to develop, not just selected individuals/families. As Sampson et al. (1997) show, neighborhoods that are equally poor can have different levels of crime as a result of differing "collective efficacy," their term for the trust and values that neighbors share. The connections between neighbors enhance their safety since they will act on each other's behalf and feel a shared sense of values.

Individuals and community-based organizations' connections with the community, or "social capital," have a similar impact, increasing the level of safety throughout the neighborhood (Lederman et al. 2002). The networks they create sustain neighborliness, and thus help residents work together for their own safety by being able to call upon others to support them. These ties act in the opposite manner to personal security decisions, such as buying a gun or shuttering your house, which could limit your connectedness and networking.

In this chapter we examine the role of safety by first exploring subjective and objective evidence on safety and crime; second, discussing changing approaches to policing; third, considering how scholars have defined the role of safety in community well-being; and last, proposing how by using social capital and collective efficacy the field might better understand safety as an measure of community well-being, including some recommendations for further research. Following the work of Kim and Lee (2014), we focus on the neighborhood scale. We recognize, as they do, that communities can now stretch far and wide due to the development of digital communications and autocentric urban settlements, yet most people still have some connection to the geographic place where they reside, and they often imagine the world through events that happen in that space.

Measures of Well-Being, Fear, and Safety

Scholars of CWB have long asked individuals if they feel safe as part of the subjective indicators of their well-being. As Kim et al. (2014) remind us, a number of surveys and indexes have been developed over the last decade to measure various definitions of individual and community well-being. In England, for instance, a recent survey found that even though crime rates in most places have continued to decline, just under a quarter of respondents still felt unsafe walking in their neighborhood at night (Self et al. 2012).

This paper builds on the work of Sung and Phillips (2014), who have created a new framework for community well-being using community development theories. They argue that "community well-being is a comprehensive concept covering other related life and community concepts" that is measured by "peoples' perceived feeling and evaluation of their life circumstances, but also objective indices such as crime, poverty, and voter rate." Community well-being, thus, is defined as "comprehensive and integrated concepts developed by synthesizing research constructs related to residents' perceptions of the community, residents' needs fulfillment, observable community conditions, and the social and cultural context of the community." Using community development theories, they create "a framework of community well-being, which consists of four major community domains," human, economic, social, and environmental. Our focus, safety, fits into this last domain.

Many scholars discuss the specific definitions of community well-being, and the indicators for measuring its presence (Sung and Phillips 2014; Kee and Nam 2014; Kim and Lee 2013; Kim et al. 2014). In this section, we are not trying to add to these multiple efforts. Instead, we wish only to demonstrate that crime is both a perceptional and an objective reality, with measures of public safety often being highly rated as concerns of urban residents, even as crime rates vary.

For example, as one of many such surveys, the 2007 Pew Global Survey results suggest the pervasive nature of the fear of crime (Pew Research Center 2007). In thirty-three of 47 countries polled, crime and corruption stood out as top fears of respondents. While crime itself and the fear of crime has been diminishing in many places given improved economic conditions and stronger social structures, a stunning number of people worldwide report they are afraid in their neighborhoods.

In their summary of the answers to the standard fear question—is there an area near your home where you are afraid to walk alone at night—Pew researchers related that even the wealthiest and seemingly safest countries, such as France and Canada, had response rates of 1 in 4 or 1 in 3 (see Table 6.1). Of the 45 countries for which they provided response rates, in only four (Egypt, Jordan, Indonesia and India) did fewer than 20 % of respondents answer yes. Conversely, in Central

Table 6.1 Homicides by region, 2012 or latest year

Region	Number	Rate
Americas	157,000	16.3
Africa	135,000	12.5
Asia	122,000	2.9
Europe	22,000	3.0
Oceania	1100	3.0

Source Adapted from UNODC Homicide Statistics (2013)

America, over 50 % of respondents did so. Finally, Pew researchers noted that women were almost always more concerned about walking at night alone than men. For instance, they reported that while 18 % of U.S. men did not feel safe, 42 % of women did so.

Just as Krekel and Poprawe found that crime had a negative impact on life satisfaction, Cornaglia examine the impact of fear of crime on the cost to individuals and Australian society. They recognize that American studies (Kling et al. 2001, 2004) have shown that people were willing to move out of public housing and risk changing neighborhoods due at least partially to fear of crime. They move this literature forward by trying to calculate the cost to mental well-being of fear of victimization, essentially fear of crime. They found that violent crime, once again, provoked the most fear, and held the most cost for society.

For Many People, the World Is not Safe

When Rath et al. (2010: 94) turn from individual to community well-being, the first issue they discuss is safety and security. They recognize that when someone doesn't feel safe, "it is difficult to have thriving well-being." Many researchers have confirmed their conclusion, that millions of people worldwide do not feel safe leading to lowered well-being (Lederman et al. 2002; Kuroki 2013). Indeed, as recent events on the southern U.S. border have dramatically shown as we write this chapter, crime and its consequences are a tragic reality for many Central American young people today (Preston and Archibold 2014).

Comparing crime rates across countries is extremely difficult (e.g., Bier 2013). However, international homicide rates are more comparable. Using these rates, we can see that crime is very uneven worldwide, with some places having dramatically more or fewer homicides. Even with the caution that homicide rates do not necessarily reflect the total property and personal crime rates for a society, Table 6.2 shows violence claims hundreds of thousands of lives each year, and creates a climate of fear for residents of these high crime countries.

As the United Nations reports, over 437,000 people were homicide victims in 2012 (or the latest reporting year), with the most occurring in the Americas, followed closely by Africa and Asia (UNODC 2013: 21). In striking contrast, Europe had only 22,000 homicides. To fully understand the role of crime in society we need to consider not just the total number of homicides, but also the homicide rate, a weighted calculation based on the number of homicides and the country's population, so we can see how homicides compare across regions. As a result, Europe has a very low rate (3.0 homicides per 100,000 people), but Asia, which has a high number of homicides, actually has a lower rate of homicide (2.9).

The results in the Americas and Africa under either calculation are tragic (UNODC 2013: 22). Africa has a homicide rate roughly 4 times higher than Europe or Asia (12.5), which is just double the global rate (6.2). The Americas are even more devastating, with a rate of 16.3, almost 5.5 times Europe, Asia, and Oceania

Table 6.2   Fear by selected country, 2007[a]

Country	Percent saying yes (%)	Country	Percent saying yes (%)
Venezuela	84	South Korea	30
South Africa	80	United States	30
Kenya	69	Malaysia	29
Brazil	64	France	29
Mexico	50	Canada	25
Poland	43	China	21
Italy	37	Kuwait	21
Tanzania	35	India	19

[a]Percent answering yes to: Is there an area near your home where you would be afraid to walk alone at night?
Source Pew Research Global Attitudes Project (2007)

(3). Perhaps a surprise to some, the Americas homicide rate is not driven by the United States, whose homicide rate is actually quite low compared to its southern neighbors in Central and South America, and the Caribbean. Honduras' homicide rate is 30 times the Europe and Asia homicide rate of roughly 3 per 100,000. Mexico has a rate of 21.5 (7 times Europe), yet ranks fourth in Central America after Honduras, Belize (44.7), and El Salvador (41.2) (UNODC 2013: 24). Such terrifying rates are one reason for the dramatic illegal exodus of young people from these countries to the United States (Preston and Archibold 2014).

Cross international metropolitan data is much harder to find. However, studies in the U.S. have suggested that more directly related to neighborhood safety, residents of larger cities are more likely to be a victim of a crime than those living in smaller cities and towns (Glaeser and Sacerdote 1999). Using crime rates from the 1990s, which admittedly have dropped dramatically in the period since their study, Glaeser and Sacerdote (1999) calculated that residents of Los Angeles and New York City, for instance, were 4 times as likely to experience a property crime, and 2.5 times more likely to experience a violent crime than individuals in smaller cities. This study, and others like it suggest, while crime occurs worldwide, and is a pervasive reality of urban life, not everyone experiences it equally or that it occurs randomly. Class, race/ethnicity, gender, and place matter with crime as they do in other social environmental realities.

Americans, along with many other nationals, are fortunate that crime rates have dramatically diminished over the last generation, but the cost of crime remains high, personally, socially, and economically (Florida 2011). As crime has dropped, urban residents have reclaimed their public spaces, such as the streets of downtown Los Angeles, but the fear of crime remains an important social indicator of individual's and communities' sense of happiness and well-being (Wachs 2013).

For instance, Krekel and Poprawe have examined the affect of crime on life satisfaction (one measure of individual well-being). Using a novel dataset combining German police statistics and the German Socio-Economic Panel (SOEP), they found that "local area crime has a significantly negative impact on life satisfaction". When they delved further into the data, they discovered that almost all of the effect came from violent crimes such as the homicides we have discussed here. Finally, they found that the worries created by local area crime also increased "their worries about crime at the global level, namely in Germany as a whole." And, perception turned out to mirror reality pretty well since people living in high-crime areas were more concerned about crime, and more frequently worried. As we shall discuss below, perhaps higher social capital or increased collective efficacy might mitigate some, but not all, of these worries.

Police and the Community

The last section demonstrates the cost of both residents' fear of crime (subjective measure of well-being) and crime itself (objective measure) has on communities. So how do communities' respond? During much of the twentieth century, and in many countries around the world, the focus has not been on community responses, but on how the professional police forces acted in alliance with criminal justice agencies. However, over the last two generations, especially in the U.S., critics have argued against reliance on police as the sole, or even primary agent of safety, arguing for a partnership between community residents, the criminal justice apparatus, and the police. As these critiques of professional policing have advanced, the focus has shifted from police technologies and practices to community dynamics, leading to an emphasis on such community development and resilience mechanisms as collective efficacy and social capital.

That these community mechanisms have an impact on crime surprises some economists who hold still to Becker's pioneering argument that criminals were just another set of rational agents responding primarily to changing circumstances, such as shifting likelihoods of being caught. Acceptance of this argument led many policymakers and commentators to argue, the focus of policing should be the individual criminal, not the community setting where the criminal acts. And, during much of the last century, policing has developed a range of activities, such as rigid sentencing requirements, use of computers to identify crime clusters, and police sweeps that conform with this view.

Indeed, such a "professional" policing model became pervasive (Lasley 2012). In this model, exemplified in the U.S. by the Los Angeles Police Department, police forces used helicopters, computers, and highly trained expertise, such as that in the SWAT teams, to combat crime. They focused less on community relationships than on "chasing the radio" that brought calls in response to crime to their cars. Foot and horse patrols, which were quite common in the early century, were largely abandoned in favor of automobiles. Police experts praised the new separation between police and community as one way to limit corruption and ensure the professionalism of the police.

Since corruption had been rampant in many police forces, efforts to professionalize were often connected to those to combat such corruption (Issac and Norton

2013). Corruption remains a critical issue for police forces in the U.S. and elsewhere in the world, but as commentators recognized the consequences of exchanging corruption for an increasing distance between residents and police officers, some critics began to argue that a new model was necessary.

Momentum for such a discussion increased in the aftermath of the urban riots of the 1960s and 1970s. Police leaders questioned the effectiveness of such a sharp separation between the community and those who service them. Also, after decades of growing police forces and other public services supported by a relatively (in hindsight) generous local public finance system, budget pressures on cities began dictating less growth in police force levels even as crime rates were increasing. The professional model seemed incapable of responding to rapidly rising levels of violence and disorder. For instance, in Los Angeles, the number of homicides rose from 281 in 1967 to over 1000 in 1992 (Rubin and Faturechi 2010). While this increase was extreme, many American cities saw similar rises in homicides, and in overall crime.

As crime rates soared in the United States, other mechanisms for achieving community safety began to be considered, and one of them was, community context matters. How that context influenced crime has taken decades (and it is still not fully completed) to describe, but scholars have shown that actions by community residents, and their ability to organize is an important component of neighborhood safety. A number of experts began calling as early as the 1970s for a new style of "community policing," that combined the expertise of the police with the "community knowledge" of community residents (Kappeler and Gaines 2011; Corburn 2005). They believed that this new partnership would not only reconnect the police to the community, but would also encourage residents to engage directly in making their neighborhoods safer.

The publication of Wilson and Kelling's (1982) "broken window" theory in 1982 provided a strong push for such change, as they argued that the nuisance crimes that many police forces ignored in their focused response to major violent crimes, which are more likely to be relayed via a radio call, had led them to miss an important aspect of their civic mission, sustaining community safety not just catching criminals. While the theory has come under considerable criticism given the lack of evidence that nuisances lead directly to more serious crimes, it did serve as a strong critique of professional policing and as a call for a new style of policing that reconnected people and police (Taylor 2001; Harcourt 2001).

Quickly, though, experts began to realize that one could not simply turn community engagement on after being off for so long. They asked, what are the mechanisms through which communities are involved in protecting themselves? And, how could community residents see the wisdom of their involvement? Out of these questions, researchers began to examine the concepts of social capital and collective efficacy as indicators of those mechanisms—of the ability of residents and neighborhoods to rally, connect, and coordinate to create safer streets and places (Sampson 2012).

Opportunities for Improving Neighbors' Safety

Lochner et al. (2003: 1798) remind us "the relationships people have with each other, and that individuals within a social structure (such as a neighborhood) can draw upon to achieve certain actions" are an important element of safety. As a result, we want to contextualize the traditional measures of crime and safety by examining two constructs related to a community's sense of connectivity, social capital and collective efficacy, as additional lens into understanding how communities create more well-being.

Social Capital: "Social capital" is an increasingly popular social variable that is a set of components, typically norms, shared understandings, trust, and other factors that make relationships possible and productive (Lochner et al. 2003). Social capital can explain community differences in income, productivity, and crime. It consists of the knowledge and other resources members of a social network use to help each other, especially in relation to economic and educational opportunities, as well as social improvement. However, unlike financial capital, social capital is less tangible; it is a set of relationships that make up a network, rather than money in a bank or stocks in a public company.

Putnam (1995, 2000) famously inaugurated a new interest in social capital when he argued that it had diminished over the last century with the decline in voluntary associations, such as bowling leagues. "Bowling alone" became an international accepted phrase for the loss of community that those nonprofit/voluntary associations represented as society became more technological (e.g., watched television rather than sang around a family piano) and family life modernized (e.g., women became involved in the working world). In the years since Putnam popularized the concept, researchers have extended his arguments, asserting, for instance, that social capital may play an important role in sustaining safe neighborhoods, among other things.

Putnam further defines the concepts of bonding and bridging social capital. Bonding social capital is good for undergirding specific reciprocity and mobilizing solidarity. It creates dense networks that provide crucial social and psychological support to community members. In contrast, bridging networks "are better for linkage to external assets and for information diffusion." They can "generate broader identities and reciprocity, whereas bonding social capital bolsters our narrow selves" (Putnam 2000: 23). The distinction between "bridgingness and bondingness" reminds us of the dual nature of social capital, that it can create strong in-group solidarity that may reinforce strong out-group antagonisms. Conversely, it can bridge between disparate groups within a multicultural society, providing linkages and producing networks that could prove vital components of a democratic society. In the community-well-being and crime research, it is necessary to consider these two aspects of nature of social capital.

One difficulty surrounding social capital is the difficulty researchers have in defining it, and then measuring its components. International surveys only recently have asked questions that effectively measure the concept's components, and no standardized questions exist for cross-national surveys. In general terms, social capital is a set of norms, shared understandings, trust, and other connections that produce productive relationships (Lochner et al. 2003). While social capital is "real," it is not as tangible as financial and other capitals, meaning that measuring its presence is more challenging. Helliwell and Putnam (2004: 1436) that the central characteristic of social capital are the "dense social networks" in a neighborhood, signified by barbeques and neighborhood association and the "bonds among family, friends and neighbors, in the workplace, at church, in civic associations, perhaps even in Internet-based 'virtual communities.'" Intriguingly, while they do not include trust as part of their core definition of social capital, they recognize that "social trust," "the belief that other around you can be trusted," is a "crucial mechanism" by which social capital influences outcomes.

However, we do know that social capital does matter in affecting safety and crime. Indeed, Helliwell and Putnam (2004: 1436) state directly that those dense social networks "can deter crime ... benefiting neighbours (sic) who do not got the barbeques or belong to the associations." Akçomak and ter Weel (2008: 23) conclude in their study of social capital and crime in the Netherlands that is "associated with lower crime rates," explaining about "10 % of the observed variance in crime." The authors go on to that the willingness of residents to intervene (a critical component of collective efficacy) increases the "level of well-being in a community," and that, in turn raises the level of trust, altruistic behavior, and participation (heightening the level of social capital), all resulting in a safe community.

Collective Efficacy: Similarly, "collective efficacy" draws upon decades of sociological research, but represents a new take on the role of neighbors in assuring the safety of a place. The term was originally defined in 1997 as, "cohesion among neighborhood residents combined with shared expectations for informal social control of public space". The origins of the term come out of the variation of crime not only between nations, states, and cities, but also at the neighborhood level. In their deep study of human development in Chicago, the authors were able to create a data set that allowed them to analyze why neighborhoods with similar socio-economic status did not have the same crime rate. Their finding was that collective efficacy, shared values and a willingness to intervene to help each other, played a key role in the difference. Given the role crime plays especially in poorer neighborhoods, the finding that associations of "concentrated disadvantage and residential instability with violence are largely mediated by collective efficacy," was an important discovery.

The authors intended the new concept partly as a rebuttal of the very popular policing concept, "broken windows," since they argued that strong collective efficacy could mediate any impacts of the nuisance disorders that Wilson and Kelling (1982) believed grew into serious crime, thus creating a negative spiral affecting neighborhood safety. As Rukus and Warner (2013: 38) have summarized, Sampson and his colleagues accepted that disorder was connected to crime, but "the real drivers of crime are factors associated with collective efficacy, which include the structural characteristics of neighborhoods, neighborhood cohesion, and informal social control." Further, collective efficacy was a response to the need to better understand why some poor neighborhoods were safer than others. The work of Sampson and his colleagues showed the value of collective efficacy's components, cohesion and willingness to intervene on the behalf of others, alleviating crime through reinforced social relationships (Choi and Sloane 2012).

In the almost twenty years since the analysis was completed in Chicago, the concept has been embraced by the criminology community, but has only more recently been more widely discovered. Many studies have confirmed the primary finding of the study, while others have begun to refine the analysis (Maxwell et al. 2011). Even those who argue that collective efficacy has significant limitations still accept that different levels of community cohesion and willingness to act on the community's behalf are distinctive characteristics of a safer community.

Crime, Safety, and Community Well-Being

Mattesich and Monsey (1997, quoted by Phillips and Pittman 2009: 52) produced a synthesis of research on community building, and identified three categories of factors that influence the success of such efforts: "social, psychological, and geographic attributes of a community and its residents," "components of the process by which people attempt to build community," and "qualities of the people who organize and lead" such an effort. These categories fit nicely with the critical importance of collective efficacy and social capital in promoting positive community development.

While researchers have succeeded in defining the components and clarifying the potential roles of these two concepts, we still do not fully understand the mechanisms by which they affect safety by lowering fear of crime and crime rates. In outlining the relationship of these two concepts to reducing crime and improving community well-being, we recognize that, as our discussions above suggest, all results are preliminary. New studies will provide further insight into the community development dynamics around safety.

Indeed, some, such as Browning (2009), remind us that community cohesion also has a downside, as the bonding capital that brings groups together is similar whether in an anti-crime neighborhood group or in a youth street gang. In some neighborhoods, a "negotiated coexistence" exists between residents and offenders, diminishing the "regulatory effectiveness of collective efficacy." As Hennigan and Sloane discovered in their study of a gang suppression tactic in Los Angeles, if the tactic is not precisely implemented, it can strengthen such negative bonding and limit the effectiveness of the effort.

Even with these caveats, the interaction of community and police is central to safe neighborhoods. Maxson et al. (2003) showed that informal contact between residents and police officers significantly improved satisfaction with the police, even among residents living in high crime areas. Policymakers and police officials felt that the media was shaping people's perceptions of the police, and the researchers discovered that people's experiences, their interactions with the police, were much more influential. In other words, by actively promoting informal relationships with residents, police officials could aid the development of not only social capital and collective efficacy, but also benefit as neighbors become less distrustful of the police. Later research, such as Kochel (2012) in Trinidad and Tobago, has reinforced this finding, although has complicated it by showing that that police legitimacy does not necessarily translate into collective efficacy.

Further, Warner and Rukus (2013) recently extended earlier research on collective efficacy by arguing that "residents and neighbors alone" do not achieve the positive effects associated with the concept. They assert instead, a partnership of residents, local government, including urban planners, and private sector investment are critical to breaking the "crime nexus." They especially suggest "impact fees," funds that augment "traditional sources of government funding for … services," are positively related to a negative impact on crime rates since they increase services such as "parks, recreation, community facilities, transit and child care."

Can neighborhood leaders develop and sustain a process of improvement that overcomes the barriers to success? What the literatures on these two facilitating factors suggests is that when people are connected, when they trust each other, and when they can rely upon each other, they are more likely to succeed in creating and maintaining a community development process.

Further research might enhance our knowledge of these important relationships. First, we need more studies such as those by Kim and Lee (2013) that further clarify how we can measure community well-being, especially ones that move beyond a comprehensive set of indicators towards specific measures in topic areas, such as safety. The single measure, do you walk alone at night, is very imprecise in helping us understand people's perception of their safety and the realities of safety in their neighborhoods.

Second, we hope that the community well-being scholarly community will look specifically at the type of ways that Hennigan and Sloane (2013) tested the implementation of a specific gang suppression tactic and Rukus and Warner (2013) examined what elements of collective efficacy interacted with specific actions local and national governments can take to improve well-being and happiness. The implementation of policies and plans could be more closely connected to better understanding approaches to improving community well-being. Happiness and well-being don't just happen, as Sung and Phillips (2014) state, community development is both a process and an outcome, we need to know more about the process.

Third, Rath et al. (2010) remind us that the foundation for community well-being is such essential elements as safety. As a result, we recommend a heightened focus on trying to understand safety within a community well-being context. A safe neighborhood is a place where residents can interact, connect, and come together, using their power to mitigate some of the socio-economic disadvantages and social structural issues they confront.

Acknowledgments This work was supported by a grant from the National Research Foundation of Korea (NRF-2013S1A3A2054622). We thank the Foundation and Drs. Kee and Lee for their support. We accept all responsibility for the arguments made in this chapter.

References

Akçomak, I. S., & ter Weel, B. (2008). The impact of social capital on crime: Evidence from the Netherlands. IZA Discussion Paper No. 3603.

Bier, D. (2013). Fact-checking Ben Swann: Is the UK really 5 times more violent than the US? *The Skeptical libertarian*. Available: http://blog.skepticallibertarian.com/2013/01/12/fact-checking-ben-swann-is-the-uk-really-5-times-more-violent-than-the-us/

Browning, C. R. (2009). Illuminating the downside of social capital: Negotiated coexistence, property crime, and disorder in urban neighborhoods. *American Behavioral Science, 52*, 1556–1578.

Choi, H., & Sloane, D. C. (2012). Does working together prevent crime? Social capital, neighborhoods, and crime. In N. Brooks, K. Kieran, & G.-J. Knaap (Eds.), *The Oxford handbook of urban economics and planning* (pp. 230–247). New York: Oxford University Press.

Corburn, J. (2005). *Street science: Community knowledge and environmental health justice.* Cambridge, MA: MIT Press.

Cozes, P., & Davies, T. (2103). Crime and residential security shutters n an Australian suburb: Exploring perceptions of 'eyes on the street,' social interaction and personal safety. *Crime Prevention and Community Safety, 15*, 175–191.

Florida, R. (2011). Don't fear the city: Urban America's crime drops to the lowest rate in 40 years, *The Atlantic*. Available: http://www.theatlantic.com/national/archive/2011/05/dont-fear-the-city-urban-americas-crime-drops-to-lowest-in-40-years/239366/

Glaeser, E. L., & Sacerdote, B. (1999). Why is there more crime in cities? *Journal of Political Economy, 107*, S225–S256.

Harcourt, B. (2001). *Illusions of order: The false promise of broken windows policing.* Cambridge, Mass.: Harvard University.

Helliwell, J. F., & Putnam, R. D. (2004). The social context of well-being. *Philosophical Transactions of the Royal Society of London B, 359*, 1435–1446.

Hennigan, K., & Sloane, D. C. (2013). Improving civil gang injunctions: How implementation can affect gang dynamics, crime, and violence. *Crime and Public Policy, 12*, 7–41.

Isaac, R. M., & Norton, D. A. (2013). *Just the facts ma'am: A case study of the reversal of corruption in the LAPD.* New York: Palgrave MacMillan.

Kappeler, V. E., & Gaines, L. K. (2011). *Community policing: A contemporary perspective.* Waltham, MA: Anderson Publishing.

Kee, Y., & Nam, C. (2014). Does sense of community matter in community well-being? Working Paper, Global Forum on Evaluating Community Well-Being.

Kim, Y., & Lee, S. J. (2013). The development and application of a community well-being index in Korean metropolitan cities. *Social Indicators Research,*. doi:10.1007/s11205-013-0527-0.

Kim, Y., Kee, Y., & Lee, S. J. (2014). An analysis of the relative importance of components in measuring community well-being: Perspectives of citizens, public officials, and experts. *Social Indicators Research,*. doi:10.1007/s11205-014-0652-4.

Kling, J., Liebman, J., & Katz, L. (2001). Bullets don't got no name: Consequences of fear in the ghetto. Joint Center on Poverty Research, Working Paper 225.

Kling, J., Liebman, J., Katz, L., & Sanbonmatsu. L. (2004). Moving to opportunity and tranquility: Neighborhood effects on adult economic self-sufficiency and health from a randomized housing voucher experiment. Kennedy School of Government Working Paper, No. RWP04-035.

Kochel, T. R. (2012). Can police legitimacy promote collective efficacy? *Justice Quarterly, 29*, 384–419.

Kurkoi, M. (2013). Crime victimization and subjective well-being: Evidence from happiness data (Japan). *Journal of Happiness Studies, 14*, 783–794.

Lasley, J. (2012). *Los Angeles police department meltdown: The fall of the professional-reform model of policing*. Boca Raton, FL: CRC Press.

Lederman, D., Loayza, N., & Menédez, A. M. (2002). Violent crime: does social capital matter? *Economic Development and Cultural Change, 50*, 509–539.

Lochner, K., Kawachi, I., Brennan, R. T., & Buka, S. L. (2003). Social capital and neighborhood mortality rates in Chicago. *Social Science and Medicine, 56*, 1797–1805.

Mattessich, P. W., & Monsey, B. (1997). *Community building: What makes it work: A review of factors influencing successful community building*. St. Paul, MN: Wilder Publishing Center.

Maxson, C., Hennigan, K., & Sloane, D. C. (2003). Getting residents feedback and participation. *NIJ Journal, 250*, 43–45.

Maxwell, C. D., Garner, J. H., & Skogan, W. G. (2011). Collective efficacy and criminal behavior in Chicago, 1995–2004. Final Report for the NJCJRS. Available: https://www.ncjrs.gov/App/Publications/abstract.aspx?ID=257130

Pew Research Center. (2007, July 24). Global opinion trends 2002–2007: A rising tide lifts mood in the developing world. Washington, D.C.: Pew Global Attitudes Project.

Phillips, R., & Pittman, R. H. (2009). *An introduction to community development*. New York: Routledge.

Preston, J., & Archibold, R. C. (2014, June 21). U.S. moves to stop surge in illegal immigration. *New York Times*, A12.

Putnam, R. (1995). Bowling alone: America's declining social capital. *Journal of Democracy, 6*, 65–78.

Putnam, R. (2000). *Bowling alone: The collapse and revival of American community*. New York: Simon and Schuester.

Rath, T., Harter, J., & Harter, J. K. (2010). *Well-being: The five essential elements*. New York: Gallup Press.

Rubin, J., & Faturechi, R. (2010, December 26). Killings in L.A. drop to 1967 levels. *Los Angeles Times*. Available: http://articles.latimes.com/2010/dec/26/local/la-me-la-crime-20101217

Rukus, J., & Warner, M. E. (2013). Crime rates and collective efficacy: The role of family friendly planning. *Cities, 31*, 37–46.

Sampson, R. (2012). *Great American city: Chicago and the enduring neighborhood effect*. Chicago: University of Chicago.

Sampson, R., Raudenbush, S. W., & Earls, F. (1997). Neighborhoods and violent crime: A multi-level study of collective efficacy. *Science, 277*, 918–924.

Self, A., Thomas, J., & Randall, C. (2012, November 20). *Measuring national well-being: Life in the UK, 2012*. London: Office for National Statistics.

Sung, K., & Phillips, R. (2014). Community well-being, community development, and theory: Conceptualizing a relational framework. Working Paper, Global Forum on Evaluating Community Well-Being.

Taylor, R. B. (2001). *Breaking away from broken windows: Baltimore neighborhoods and the nationwide fight against crime, grime, fear, and decline*. Boulder, CO: Westview Press.

United Nations Office of Drugs and Crime (UNODC). (2013). Global study on homicide: Trends, contexts, and data. Available: http://www.unodc.org/documents/gsh/pdfs/2014_GLOBAL_HOMICIDE_BOOK_web.pdf

Wachs, M. (2013). Turning cities inside out: Transportation and the resurgence of downtowns in North America. *Transportation, 40*, 1159–1172.

Wilson, J. Q., & Kelling, G. (1982). Broken windows. In R. LeGates & F. Stout (Eds.), *The City Reader* (pp. 256–265). New York: Routledge.